I0753744

PAINTING IN CAPPADOCIA

A GUIDE TO THE SITES AND BYZANTINE CHURCH DECORATION

CECILY HENNESSY

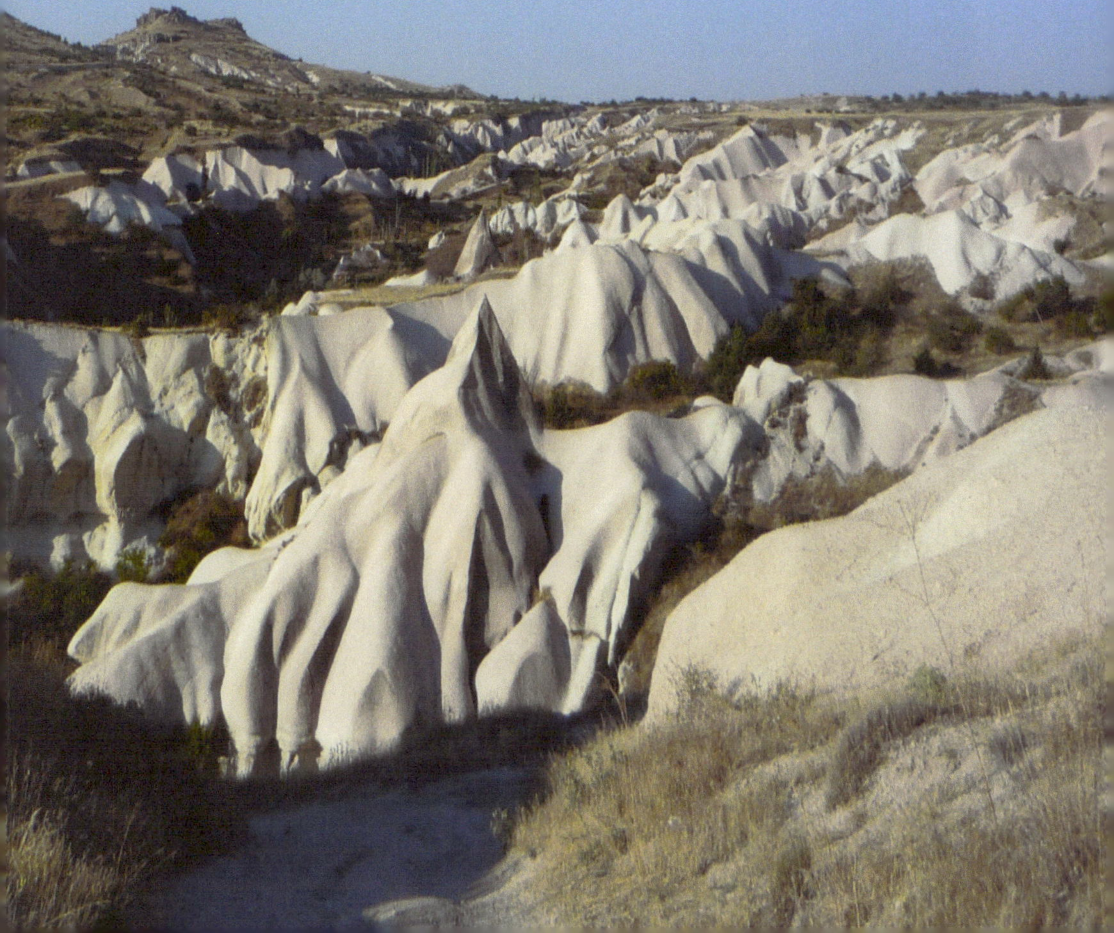

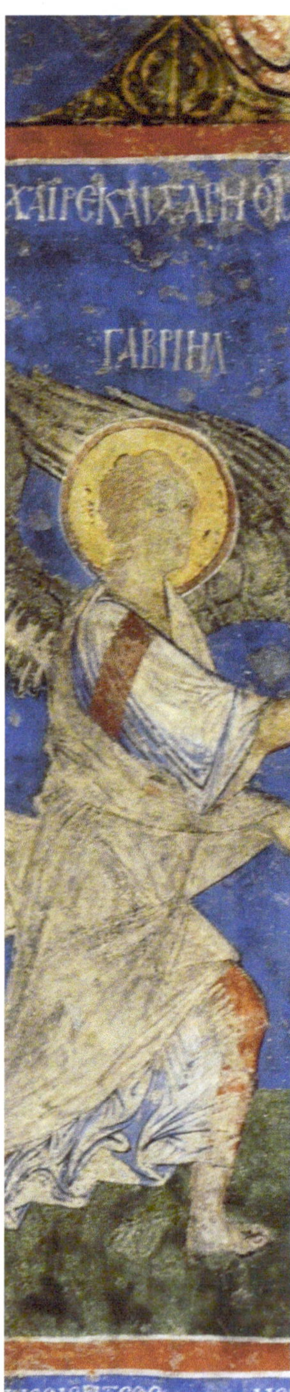

Published by Cecily Hennessy Publications.
Second edition, 2014.

Copyright © Cecily Hennessy, 2013.

All rights reserved.

Design by Simon Firullo.

Photographs by Cecily Hennessy.

Deepest thanks to Simon Firullo for the design and for layout assistance. Sincere thanks too to Antony Eastmond, Lyn Rodley, Inigo de la Rocha, Penny Ericson, Jean Williams, Selah Hennessy, Sarah Lescht and Petra Williams Lescht.

ISBN 978-0-9576628-0-3

Front end paper: El Nazar kilise, Göreme; St Stephen kilise, Cemil; Eski Gümüsler; Ağaç Altı kilise, Tokalı kilise, Göreme; Göreme chamber; back end paper: Tokalı kilise, Göreme; title page: Göreme valley; front matter page: Angel Gabriel, Annunciation, Tokalı Kilise, Göreme; contents page, Deacon, Eski Gümüsler.

PAINTING IN CAPPADOCIA

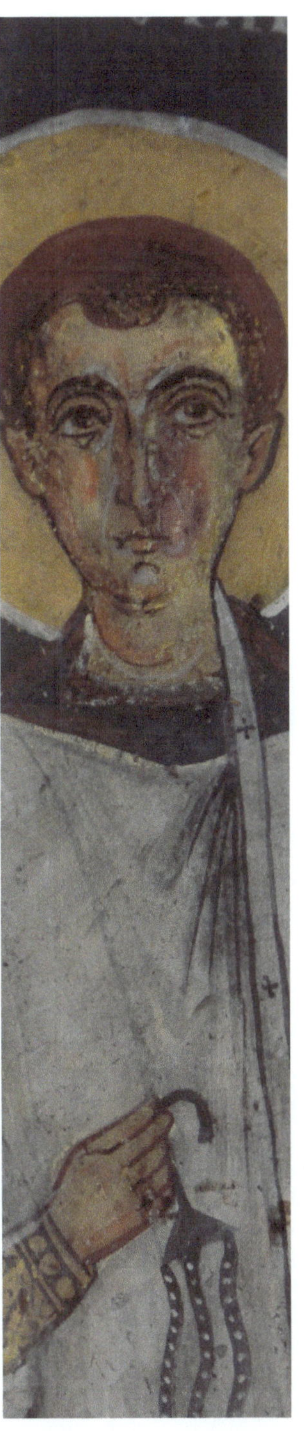

PREFACE

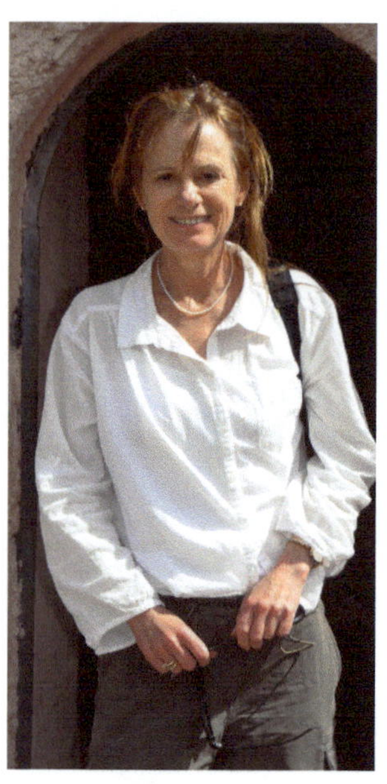

Cecily Hennessy

Painting in Cappadocia explores the more accessible and the most fascinating painted Byzantine churches in Cappadocia in central Turkey. This physically stunning area with arresting volcanic rock formations houses a myriad caves. These have been used for millennia to provide shelter for the local people and their animals, but also from the early Christian period were made into places of worship. Many of these rock cut churches were decorated with paintings made by the monks themselves, by local artists, or by artists brought from other centres, such as Constantinople.

This book is designed to appeal to the casual visitor to the area as well as those seeking a more informed art-historical understanding of the material. It is organised geographically, so it serves as a travel guide with sites close to each other grouped together. It gives both historical and art-historical information, encouraging exploration and questioning. It also aims to demonstrate how to interpret a building and how to read and understand the subject matter and meaning in a painting.

CHAPTER ONE:

INTRODUCTION

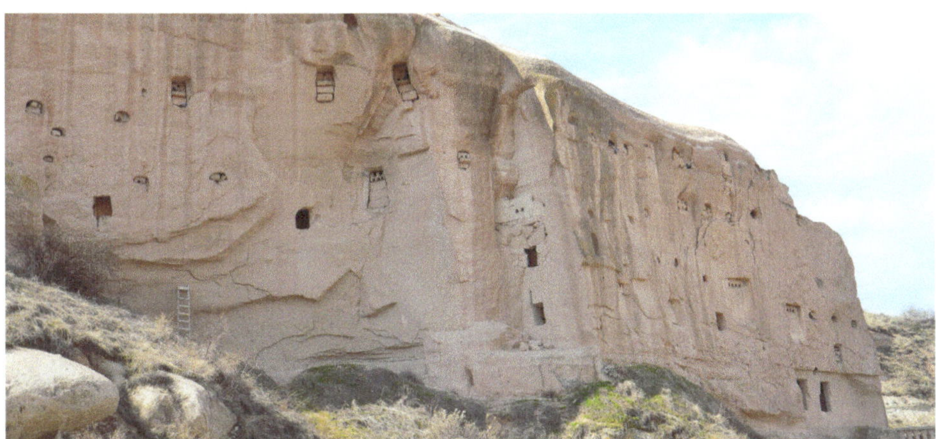

Caves and pigeon houses by Çavuşin old village

The Cappadocian landscape, with its beauty and strangeness, has evolved over several million years. Striking rock formations have been gradually shaped by nature and subsequently ingeniously fashioned by men, women and children. Wide valleys have outcrops of volcanic rock, studded with both natural and excavated caves which were dug out from early times to house the local people along with their cattle and pigeons. Domestic caves are plain in comparison with the churches and monasteries, similarly dug out of the rock, many of which are painted with vivid Christian images, narrative depictions from the Old and New Testaments as well as portraits of saints, local donors, the monks who lived in the valleys and even of the Byzantine emperor and his family. It is these paintings which are the focus of this book.

Cappadocia was wealthy and well-travelled, situated on an important trade route extending from Constantinople through Caesarea (modern Kayseri) and on to the east. It was well administered following the system set up by the Romans and from the early fourth century CE ruled from Constantinople, the capital of the Roman empire in the east (modern Istanbul). Cappadocia was a great centre of Christianity in the third and fourth centuries CE when this new religion was being defined. Several early saints and religious leaders lived in the area and were in close touch with the crucially formative events occurring in Rome, Antioch and in other important Christian centres.

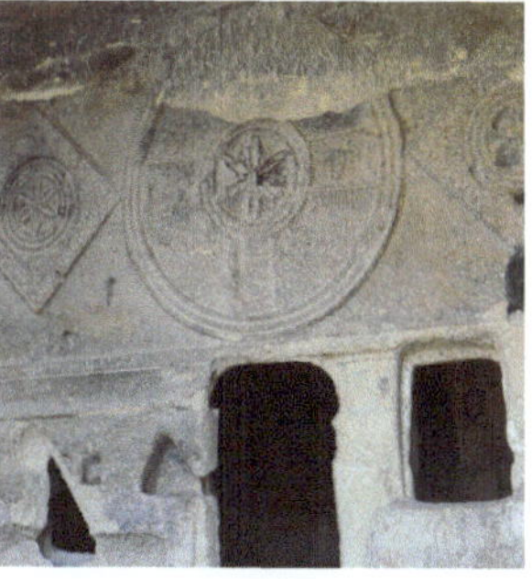

Carved wall, Church of St John, Çavuşin, about fifth century

Several impressive **Christian buildings** were established in the first centuries of Christianity, such as Saint Basil's centre of worship and philanthropy near Caesarea. Until the middle of the seventh century, the region was politically secure although few buildings or decoration survive from then. One important church still retaining its early form is St John in Çavuşin (page 22).

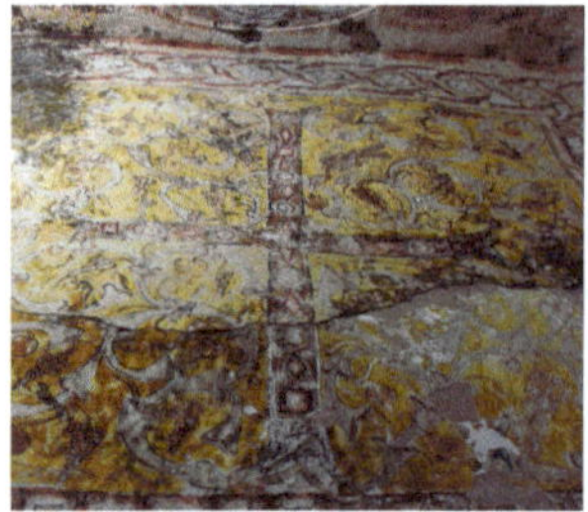

Ceiling decoration, St Stephen, Cemil (page 42)

Non-figural decoration with geometrical or floral designs is often thought to date from the period known as Iconoclasm. A controversial topic, these paintings are particularly hard to date.

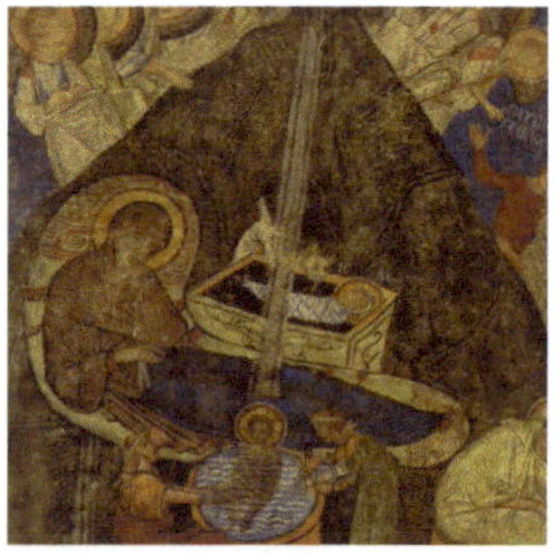

Nativity, Tokalı Kilise, New Church, Göreme (page 48)

The decoration of the Cappadocian churches drew skilled **artists** from the capital of the Byzantine empire, Constantinople, as well as local artists who evolved provincial styles and iconography.

When the Arab invasions began in 642 the area became unsettled and the Christian communities retreated, although it appears that some of the monks entrenched and carried on their secluded devotional lives in monasteries deep in the valleys. During two periods known as Iconoclasm, from 726-787 and from 815-843, the portrayal of figures in religious art was banned by the emperors.

After Iconoclasm, in the late-ninth, tenth and eleventh centuries, Cappadocia again came under Byzantine control. It was populated with various groups of people from the Byzantine empire as well as from Armenia and Syria, and the number of churches and the richness of some of the paintings indicates a flourishing of Christian culture.

In 1071 the Turkish Islamic tribe of the Seljuks defeated the Byzantine emperor at the battle of Manzikert. The Sultanate in Konya controlled Cappadocia until the middle of the thirteenth century when it was taken over by the Mongols, followed by Turcoman tribes and eventually by the Ottoman forces. During the Seljuk period, Christians continued to live in Cappadocia and there is some painting from this time, but in general the excavating and decorating of churches was less prevalent.

Little wall painting survives from this time beyond Cappadocia, so the painted churches of Cappadocia are both crucial and fascinating in recording the techniques, style and iconography of wall painting from the middle Byzantine period (843-1261).

Important early Christian leaders

Influential Christians from Cappadocia include Basil the Great, Bishop of Caesarea (330-379), who established communal monasticism (before him monks had usually lived in isolation), Basil's brother, Gregory, Bishop of Nyssa (c. 335-post 394), and their close friend, Gregory of Nazianzos (c. 330-c. 390), who became archbishop after chairing the church council in Constantinople in 381 in which the Nycene creed was revised.

CHAPTER TWO:

THE GÖREME VALLEY

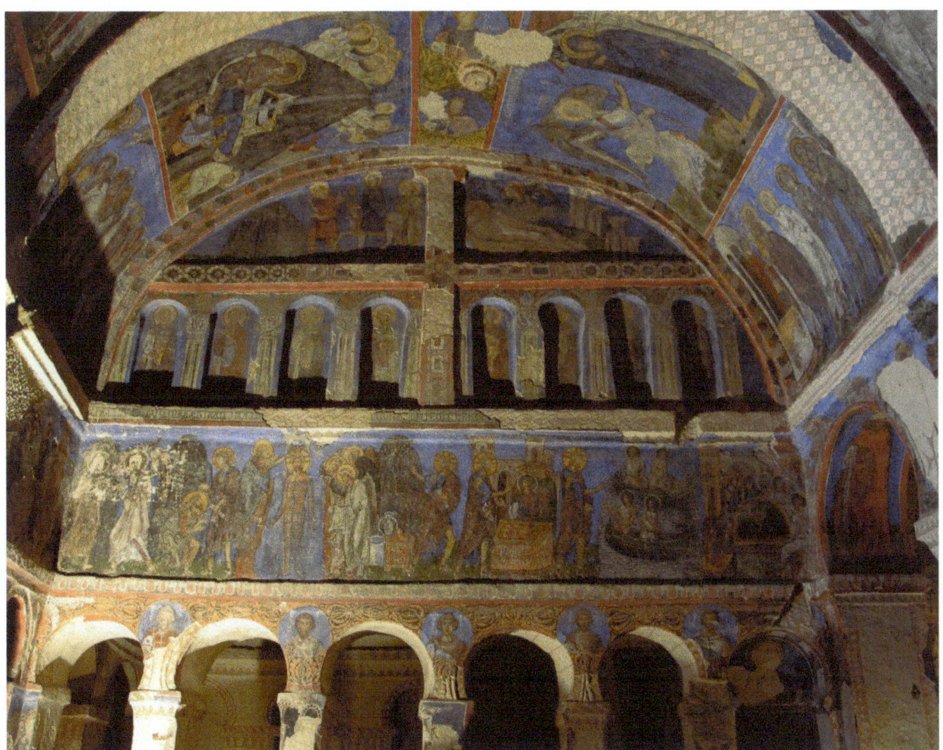

THE OPEN AIR MUSEUM

The Göreme valley is the best known and most visited area of Cappadocia and is now a UNESCO world heritage site. It has some thirty churches, many of which have unusual patterned designs and beautifully painted scenes from the bible, particularly focusing on the life of Christ and on stories from Christian traditions about the lives of saints. The main group of churches are presented as an 'open air museum'.

Tokalı Kilise (Buckle church)

Tokalı Old Church

The first church is the Old Church. As you enter from the narthex, imagine that there is a wall at the far end, forming the apse of a single nave church. This wall was later knocked through when the New Church was excavated.

Tokalı Kilise, New Church, Göreme

The most elaborate and sophisticated painted church in the 'open air museum' is **Tokalı kilise**, is set on its own nearby and is included in the same entry fee. This church has three parts, the Lower Church, the Old Church and the New Church Although the front wall has disappeared, part of the narthex or vestibule can be seen as you enter. It is a barrel vaulted space with paintings of the Pentecost; six of the apostles can be seen seated on thrones in the vault.

The paintings in **Tokalı Old Church** are some of the finest early ones in Cappadocia and appear to have been made by artists who also worked together at Ayvali church in Güllü Dere (page 24), where an inscription suggests a date of 913-20. Due to the style and sophistication of the painting, art historians think that the artists were not local but perhaps came from Constantinople.

The vault of the Old Church is painted with narrative scenes from both the New Testament and from apocryphal writings showing events in the lives of the Virgin and Christ. The paintings form a narrative with scenes arranged in chronological order starting in the top of the vault on the south side (the side on your right as you enter) at the east end (the far end). They run around the building in a clockwise direction, making two circuits and end at the northeast corner. These scenes appear over and over again in Cappadocian churches (figures 1-2).

Below the narrative scenes on the north wall is a row of standing saints, with the large figure of Saint Hieron at the east end (he was painted later). Many of the saints found depicted in Cappadocian churches are the same as found elsewhere in the Byzantine world.

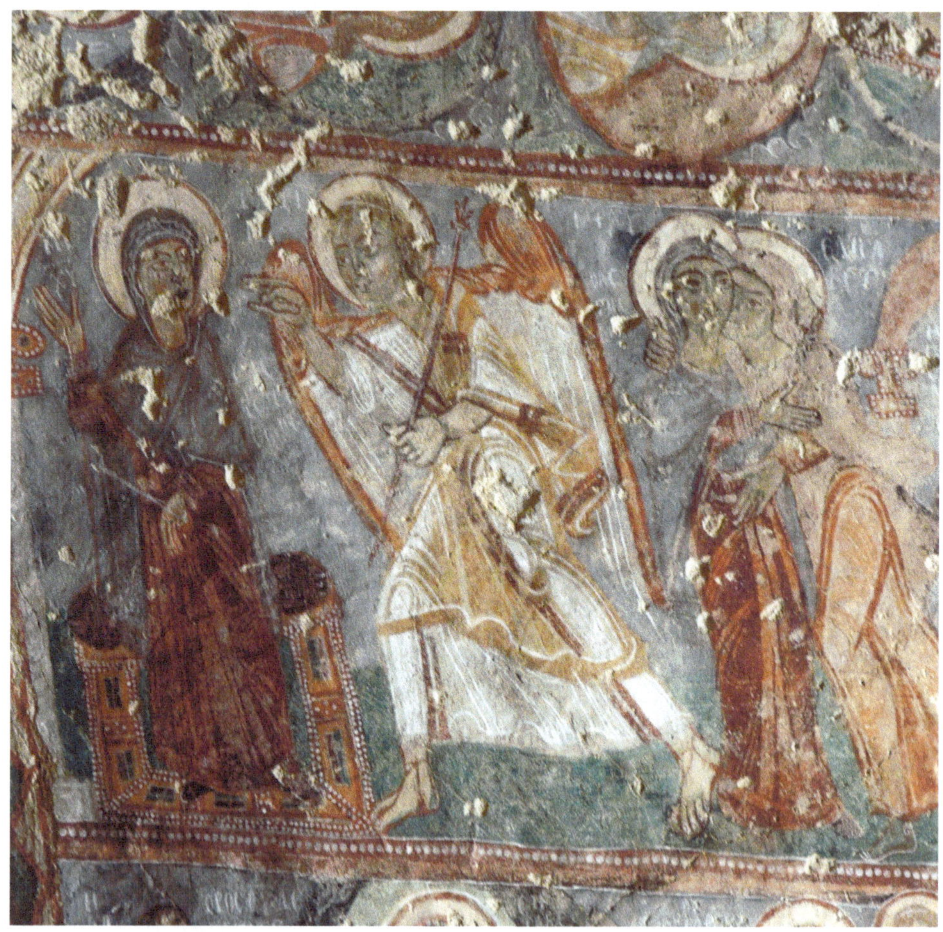

Annunciation and Visitation, ceiling vault, Tokalı Kilise, Old Church, Göreme

Paintings

Who made the paintings?

We know very little about the artists who worked in Cappadocia, but their skills ranged from the most straightforward to the most sophisticated. Some of the paintings were seemingly made by the monks themselves, such as the sketched figures at Karabaş kilise in the Soğanlı valley (page 28).Occasionally, an artist has signed his name, but this is very unusual. Some of the very fine paintings also may have been painted by monks, perhaps local ones. Basil the Great encouraged manual labour among monks and the creation of a beautiful space to the honour of God would be a laudable activity. Extensive painting programmes must have been made by a team of painters, sometimes referred to as a workshop. Often where two or more artists work together the various tasks are allocated so that one, usually the master, will sketch out the programme and perhaps paint the faces and more important areas and assistants will paint the lesser figures and the backgrounds. In a few cases, it is clear that the same workshop worked on more than one church, such as at Ayvali kilise (page 24) and Tokalı Old Church (page 7) and at the three 'column churches' in Göreme, Karanlık, Çarıklı and Elmalı kiliseler. The paintings are remarkably homogenous, but it has been suggested that Karanlık kilise was painted first with the master artist overseeing the work and that the other two were painted later by other members of the workshop. Although they adopt the same style and very similar choice of scenes, certain exaggerations and inaccuracies suggest less expertise. It is also thought that a model was used from which the images were selected. Evidence of a model is usually discerned if small mistakes are made, perhaps the presence of a halo with no body or an extra foot, or a miscopied inscription.

The artists were not necessarily local and the finest painting is often thought to be made by artists from other important Byzantine centres, particularly Constantinople. Comparisons are sometimes made with manuscripts, as few wall paintings from this period remain in Istanbul.

Painting technique

In many churches, the paint is applied directly onto the cave face, particularly where simple geometric motifs are in red or green pigment, as at St Barbara in Göreme (page 16). The plainest of these designs may well have been made by the carver and not by a painter, with the intention of demarking the area as a Christian site. In other cases geometric patterns are painted on top of plaster, as at St Stephen in Cemil (page 42), and are clearly a finished decorative programme. Occasionally only certain areas of a chapel were plastered and painted, with a focus on the most important areas, usually the apse and perhaps a burial niche. At times lime wash was put straight onto the rock with no plaster, as in the Old Church at Tokalı kilise. When plaster was used, the surface was covered with plaster, sometimes combined with sand and plant stems or straw which helps prevent shrinkage. The designs were usually sketched with red ochre paint on the plaster, which served as a guide to the final image. Sometimes the paintings were done in fresco technique, where the plaster is still wet when the paint is applied. The paint bonds with the plaster and is therefore embedded in it. This technique was often used in combination with the secco technique, where the paint is applied onto a dry wall. In both cases, the pigments were mixed with a water soluble binder, often egg yolk. Traditionally, the highest parts of the building were painted first, and the scaffolding then gradually taken down in order to paint the lower areas. It is possible sometimes to see where the plaster has been laid in registers, called pontate, starting with the top and then moving down the walls.

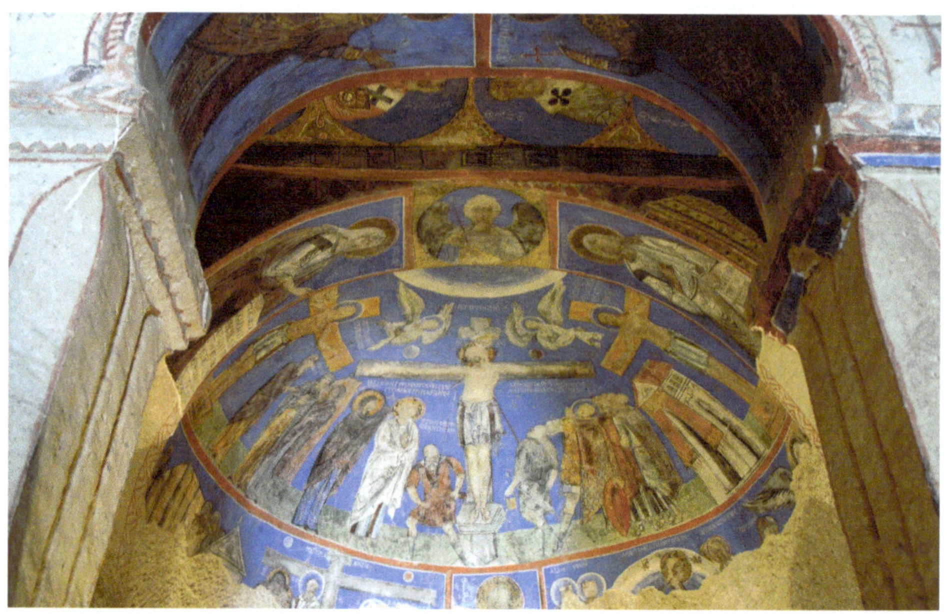

Crucifixion, apse, Tokalı kilise, New Church, Göreme

This depiction of the **Crucifixion** shows how the **painting style** had changed in just half a century, with the figures becoming more elongated and graceful and the scenes more complex in their settings and arrangement. The **artists** most probably came from Constantinople, had access to costly paints and brought with them the most up to date, superbly refined style.

Tokalı New Church

The space beyond the barrel vaulted nave is the New Church. Its date can also be determined, since the scene of the Ascension and Benediction in the vault is copied at the Church of Nikephoros Phokas (page 23), which can be dated to 963-9. So this church was probably decorated shortly before then. The Old Church had therefore been painted for perhaps 50 years when it was extended. The old paintings were preserved, presumably because they were highly valued. The site must have had great significance to be extended in such an elaborate and costly way. There is no parallel in Cappadocia in terms of its sophistication, and its patrons must have had ample resources.

The Sense of Seeing

Now a few of the churches have electric lighting, which makes a huge difference to the way you view the paintings as the lights tend to spotlight certain images. The strength of the sun varies greatly during the day and throughout the year. Particularly with churches with no artificial lighting, if you visit twice at different times you will notice how much your impression of the building changes. As the churches are mostly excavated caves, the light is very limited. Where the ceilings or walls have fallen down or been eroded, more light enters the internal spaces, but these churches were for the most part very dark spaces, lit only by candles, which were very expensive, or more usually by oil lamps, which usually hung between arches or were placed in niches, their soot darkening the nearby stone. The light thrown by them was dim and inconstant, flickering and tinged with a yellowing light.

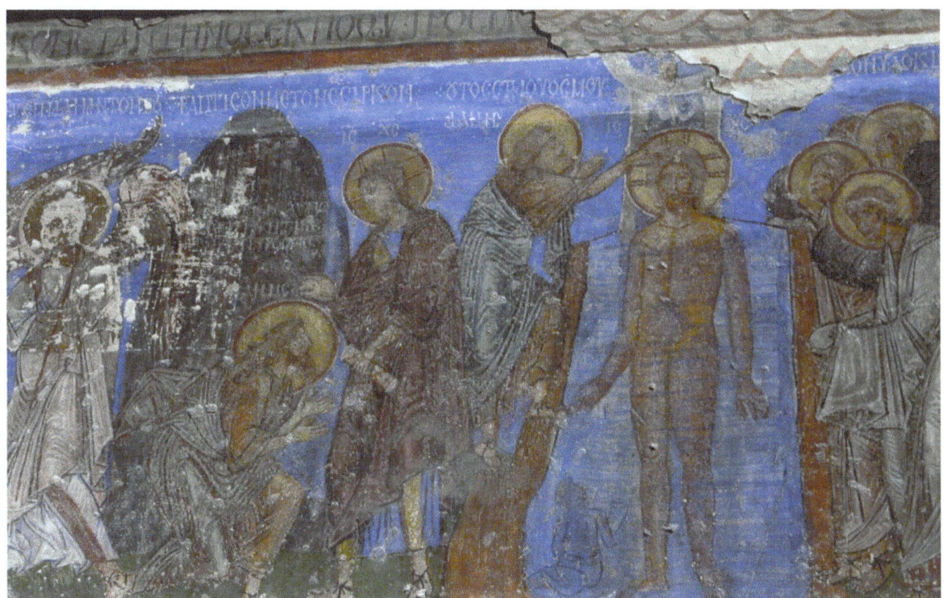

Entering the New Church one is struck by its brilliant colours and spaciousness (figure 3). With the entrance set at an angle, it is useful to move into the centre of the area in front of the main apse (the central alcove to the east decorated with the Crucifixion), and gain a sense of the expansive volumes to your left and right.

The scenes start on the east face of the vault in the north bay with the Annunciation. Below and above the left (north) apse is the Trial by Water, the Visitation and Joseph's Reproach. Moving to the north tympanum are the Dream of Joseph and the Journey to Bethlehem, set beneath the curve of the tympanum, with the Nativity on the west face of the vault, facing the Annunciation. Below here is the Adoration of the Magi. The narrative then encircles the entire nave frieze, starting by the Old Church (north side) and moving in a clockwise direction to return to the entrance to the Old Church (south side). The scenes are the Flight to Egypt, Presentation in the Temple, Christ as a Boy teaching in the Temple (this is an unusual scene), and then moving on to the north frieze, scenes with John the Baptist up to the Baptism and then the Temptation of Christ, the Calling of Matthew, the Calling of Peter, Andrew, James and John and finally, just before the corner, the Miracle at Cana. Scenes from Christ's ministry are on the spandrels between the arches on the east wall, with miracles of healing including the blind man and the man with the withered arm. These scenes continue onto the south wall with scenes from the Passion: the Raising of Lazarus, the Entry into Jerusalem, the Last Supper

Baptism and cornice inscription, Tokalı Kilise, New Church, Göreme

Inscriptions on the nave cornice and in the north apse reveal that the artist was named Nikephoros and the decoration was paid for by Leon and his father Constantine out of love for the monastery. The blue background is painted in **ultramarine** from lapis lazuli, which was very expensive and so rarely used for wall painting particularly before the thirteenth century.

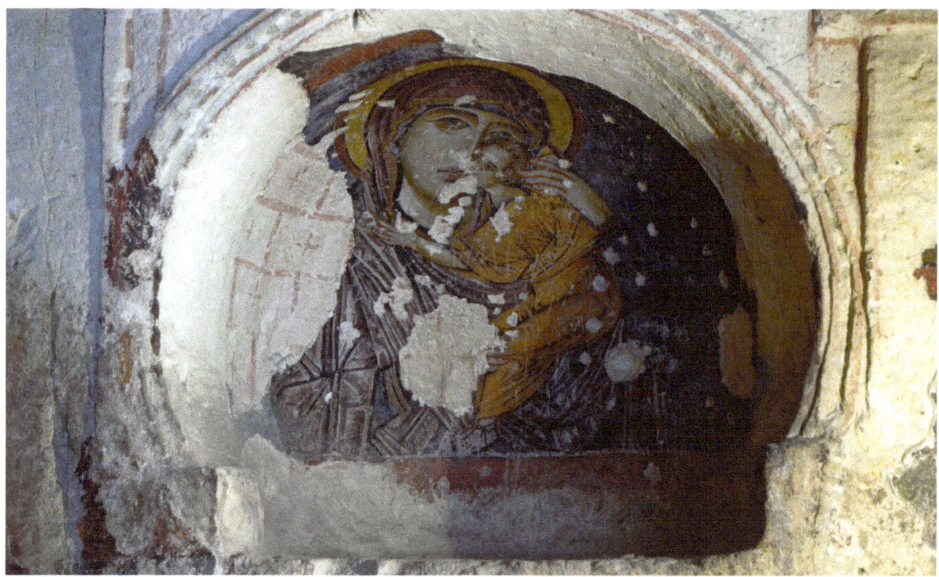

Virgin and Child, Tokalı kilise, New Church, Göreme

The **ceiling at Tokalı kilise** has a transverse barrel vault running from north to south, opening up the space. Spaciousness is also gained by the full rounded depth of the apse. The ceiling vault is demarcated by two arches, a purely decorational device which allows the nave to be divided into three bays.

The complexity of the wall surface on the north, south and west walls is created by a central register of **blind arcading** (an arcade with wall behind it), leaving registers both above and below for narrative scenes. In the north wall at ground level an arcade formed of elegant horseshoe arches leads to a small chapel with an apse. The east wall similarly has a horseshoe shaped arcade with bevelled corners separating the main vessel of the church from a passage which runs in front of the **three apses** and provides further surface for painting. Each apse has an altar and a low chancel screen separating it from the passage.

and further events from the Washing of the Disciples' Feet to Christ before Pilate. The main apse has the Crucifixion in the conch and scenes following it on the walls, from the Deposition and Entombment to the *Anastasis* or Harrowing of Hell and the Women at the Tomb. The narrative is continued in the central and south ceiling vaults with a large and triumphant Ascension in the central vault next to the Blessing of the Apostles, the Pentecost and the Mission of the Apostles. The Transfiguration is on the wall between the bema and the right apse (the *diakonikon*) and the Koimisis or Dormition on the wall between the bema and left apse (the *prothesis*).

Scenes from the life of Basil the Great appear on the north part of the west wall and on the north arcade. This is fairly unusual iconography for mural decoration, but Basil was from Cappadocia and so his life was significant here.

A niche in the east wall by the chancel screen contains a very beautiful painting of the Virgin and Child, known as the Virgin *Eleousa*, of Tenderness (illustrated above).

The Lower Church

Stairs go down from near the entrance to the Old Church to the Lower Church, which is not decorated. It was perhaps excavated at the same time as the New Church to provide a funerary chapel. Its basic shape is similar to, but smaller than, that of the New Church. With three apses, it has three aisles separated by arcades. Spaces for burials are cut into the north wall.

The rest of the 'open air museum'

After entering through the automatic gates, visitors usually start by walking to the right and proceed in an anticlockwise direction, but if you are able you might choose to go in the opposite direction, starting to the left with Çarıklı kilise and proceeding clockwise. Karanlık kilise has an additional charge but is well worth visiting and this might equally be a good place to start. The churches are given here in an order which groups them stylistically.

Karanlık kilise

This church, the finest of the painted churches in this area, is dated on stylistic grounds to the middle of the eleventh century. It is excavated high in the rock side and has a series of rooms around it, which formed the monastic buildings.

The entrance is through a horseshoe arch leading via stone steps to the barrel-vaulted narthex. The narthex is set at an angle to the church

It is tempting to walk straight through to the church but the narthex paintings merit attention. On the right or west face of the vault is a dedicatory panel, showing the Benediction of the Apostles with two kneeling figures on the left and right of Christ, named as John Entalmatikos (a title which is uncertain but perhaps indicates he was working with the patriarchate), and Genethlios. Other paintings in the narthex include an Annunciation flanking the door to the nave and various standing saints.

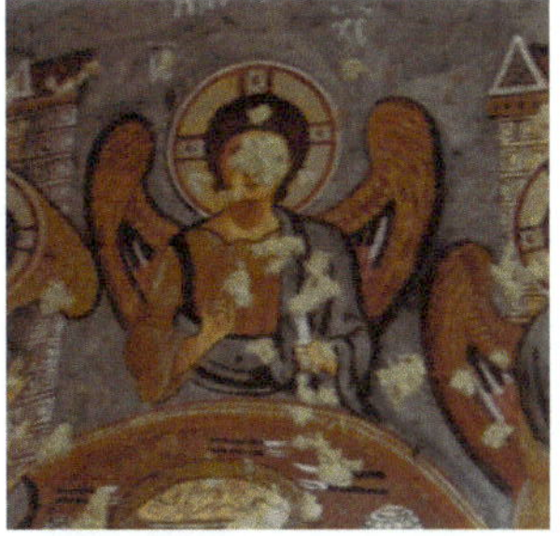

Three angels visiting Abraham, detail, Çarıklı kilise, Göreme

Karanlık, Çarıklı and Elmalı kiliseler were all painted by the same **workshop** at a similar time and are sometimes referred to as the 'column churches'. It is interesting to compare them closely and to question how the artists worked, who employed them and who decided what they should paint. This scene is from Çarıklı kilise and shows three men or angels who visited the patriarch Abraham.

To the right of the stairs up to **Karanlık kilise** are the remains of a large two storey vestibule with paintings including the Virgin and Child with angels.

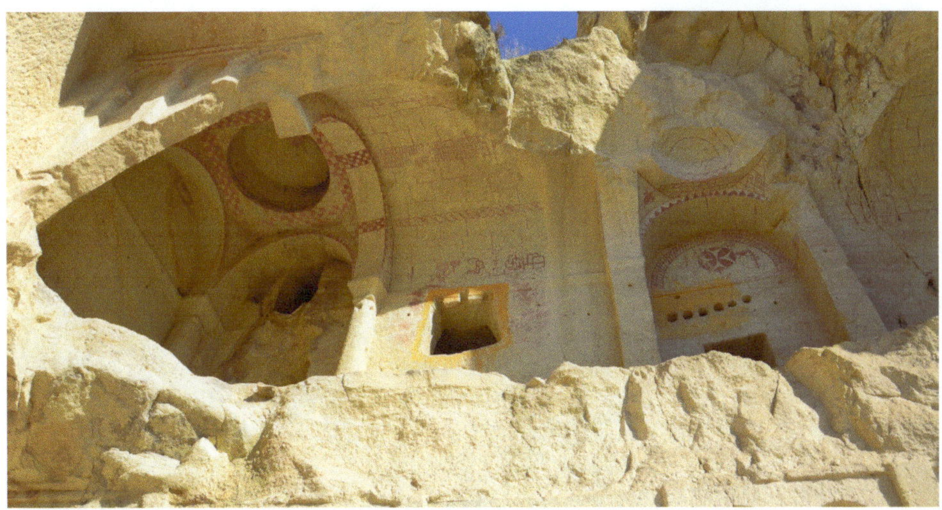

Vestibule, Karanlık kilise, Göreme

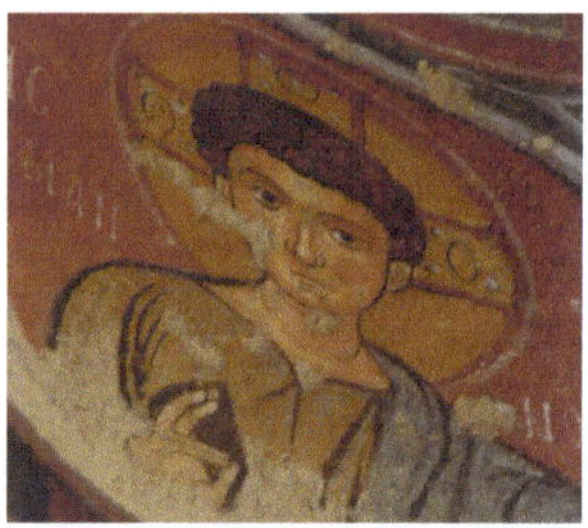

Christ Emmanuel, dome, Çarıklı kilise, Göreme

In the column churches, **Christ Pantokrator** holds a Gospel book representing his teaching and looks down from above on the believers below. Surrounding him in roundels are a host of angels and **Christ Emmanuel**, represented as a boy, as shown above. Christ Pantokrator is also in the dome near to the apse and in the apse itself, while scenes from his life fill the vaults and walls.

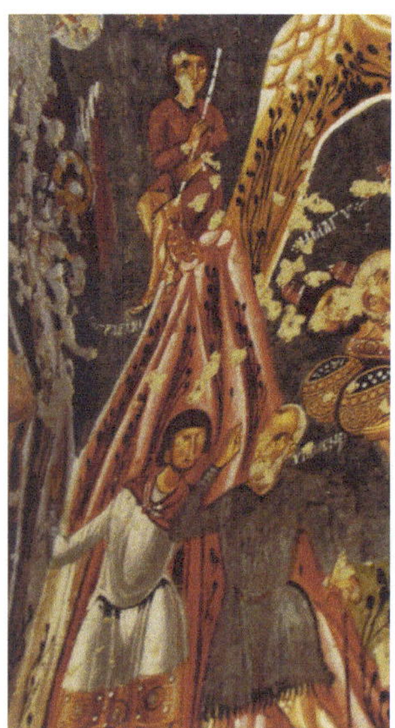

Shepherds in the scene of the Three Magi, Çarıklı kilise, Göreme

The church is of a finely proportioned cross-in-square design (see box page 20) with six-domes, a triple apse, narthex and funerary chamber. The central dome is supported on four columns, another dome is to the west of the apse and four further domes cover the corner bays.

Entering the church you are presented with a wealth of painted surface, every face decorated with richly coloured images of Christ's life and a myriad of prophets and saints. The programme was carefully planned with the highest spot, the central dome, containing a powerful bust of Christ Pantokrator, the Ruler over All.

In the apse are two further donors kneeling in front of Christ, the Virgin and John the Baptist. The inscriptions identify them as Nikephoros the Presbyter, who wears priest's clothes, and Bassianos, who seems younger. On the north and south walls of the church are the archangels Gabriel and Michael, each standing with a small, probably young, figure on either side (one is lost). These six figures, along with the two in the narthex all appear to be donors to the church, perhaps family members or close associates.

One feature of this church is the emphasis on youth and age. For instance, in pairing the standing saints on the arches, each aged saint corresponds to a youthful saint. On the soffits, the curved arches, around the central dome, a young and old figure are paired: to the east of the dome, two prophet kings, David and Solomon appear together, each dressed in imperial costume, David, white-haired and bearded, Solomon brown-haired and beardless with a delicate oval-shaped face. To the south is Jeremiah, with long grey hair, white beard, and a lined forehead, paired with Daniel (mistakenly named Solomon), appearing in Persian costume, with ruddy cheeks and a beardless face. To the north are Isaiah and Habakkuk, who has long brown hair and an oval face. In the narrative scenes too, some of the disciples are shown as particularly young. For instance, in the Last Supper, four disciples are young, John, Judas, Thomas and Philip, while Judas, again, is young in the Betrayal. Each figure is named in Greek.

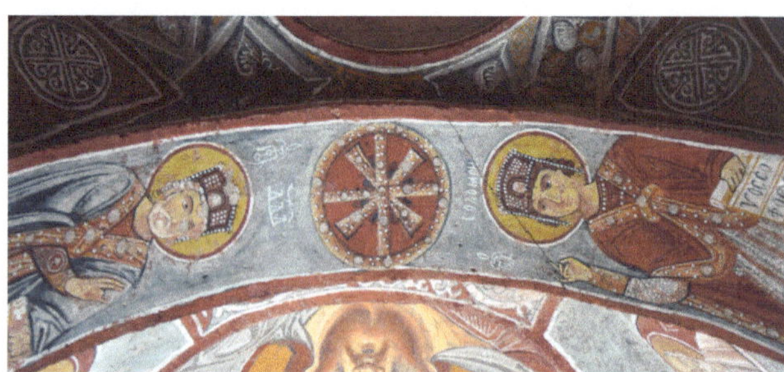

Kings David and Solomon, Çarıklı kilise, Göreme

Çarıklı kilise (Church of the Sandals)

This church is reached by steps and was excavated above a refectory and another room. The foot-shaped depressions that give this church its name are in the floor of the south arm and must be the result of excavation.

Christ Pantokrator with five archangels and Christ Emmanuel are again in the central dome, and archangels decorate the three smaller domes. The scenes from the life of Christ are very similar to those in Karanlık kilise. Here there is one donor panel on the west wall, with (probably), Simon of Cyrene (who carried Christ's cross), and three male donors, Theognostos on the left and Leon and Michael on the right. There is one Old Testament scene, the Trinity, which is on the wall above the north apse.

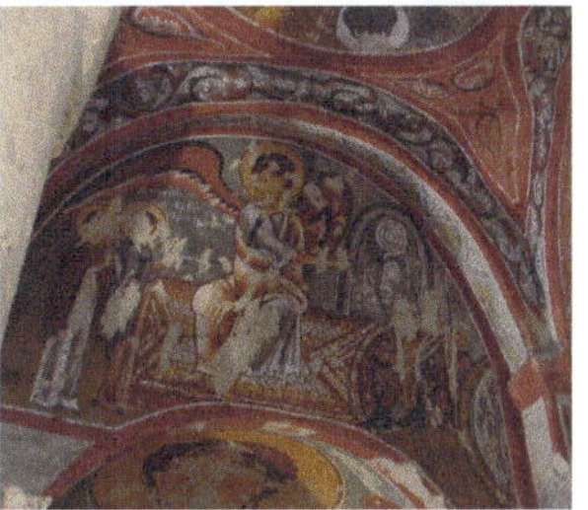

Marys at the tomb, showing an angel on Christ's tomb, Çarıklı kilise, Göreme

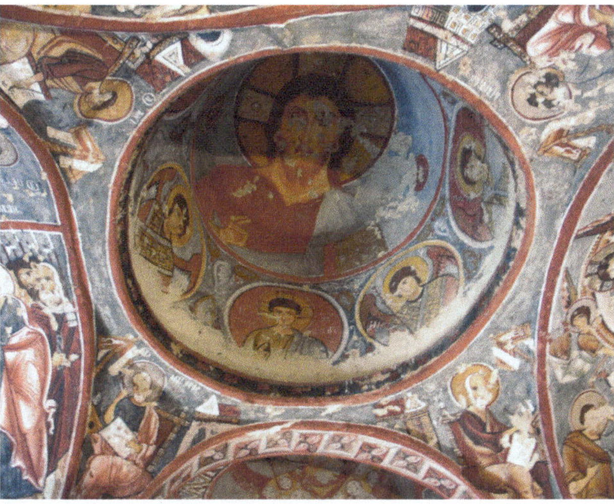

Dome, Çarıklı kilise, Göreme

Elmalı kilise (Apple Church)

This, the third of the 'column' churches, has all four columns supporting the central dome. Here the design is elaborated in a very small space with Christ Pantokrator in the main dome and archangels in the smaller ones. The decoration is very similar to that in Karanlık kilise. It now has one Old Testament scene, the Three Hebrews in the Fiery furnace, which is on the west wall.

The **design of Çarıklı kilise,** one of the 'column' churches, is modified so that it only has two columns, set at the east end. Perhaps by accident the excavators miscalculated and had no space for the two at the west end, so the central dome is supported by the west walls. Domes cover each of the three eastern bays and there are three apses.

The **style of painting** in the column churches is both highly legible and very beautiful. The background is dark blue throughout, unifying the images, which are separated by borders. In the scenes, the figures and settings are densely packed, depicted with a wonderful sense of surface decoration, as in the clothing of the three kings in the Adoration of the Magi. The bodies of the figures tend to harmonise with each other, creating graceful and concordant shapes, and the faces are sweet and serene, often placed at exquisitely charming angles. The colours are rich and varied.

Saints in imperial and foreign dress

Some saints appear in imperial dress, such as the kings from the Old Testament. David, who is usually shown with white hair and a beard, and his son Solomon, who is young and beardless, are particularly popular. Another distinctive Old Testament figure is Daniel, who is dressed in Persian costume with leggings and a Phrygian cap with the top pulled over.

It is thought that simple and often **monochrome paintings** were put in many churches as a form of protection for the buildings before the main decoration took place, but the designs at the church of St Barbara are elaborate enough to suggest they were a completed programme.

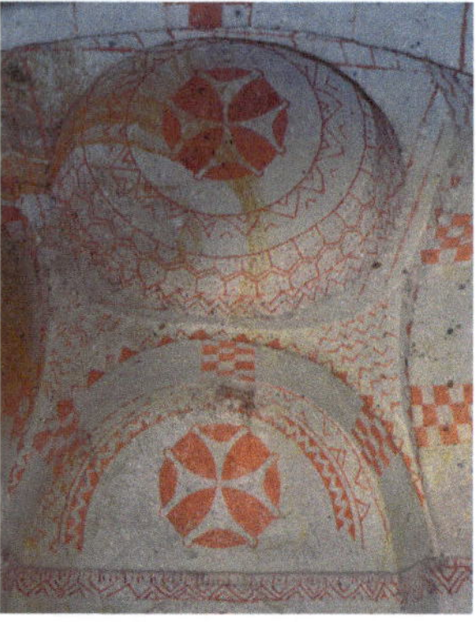

Monochrome paintings in a rock cut room, Göreme

St Barbara kilise

This church is named after the popular Byzantine saint Barbara. The plan of St Barbara is very similar to that of Çarıklı kilise, and the cross-in-square design has only two columns. When the church was first excavated it was entirely decorated with simple, mainly geometric designs in a red ochre paint. These highlight the architectural forms of the church, with a cross in the dome surrounded by abstracted palm trees which suggest paradise. The pendentives (the triangular sections supporting the dome), are picked out with triangles, and the barrel vaults in the corners are marked with lines suggesting stone work, while geometric patterns appearing like blocks of stone decorate the arches, and the capitals and tops of columns are also painted. Medallions, crosses, tree-like forms and imaginary animals are on the walls.

Later, key figures were added to the decoration in a rather rudimentary style. There is a seated Christ is in the apse, Saint Barbara on the north wall of the west arm of the cross, and two other female saints, Eirene and Catherine on the adjacent wall, and Saints Theodore and George on horses slaying the dragon on the north wall.

The inscription between Theodore and George reads, 'Lord help thy servant priest' and the one to the right 'Lord, help thy servant Leon Maroulines', suggesting that these two were patrons of the church.

Female saints

There are several female saints who are often shown grouped together, all looking young, beautiful and serene. Saint Catherine wears imperial dress as she came from an aristocratic Egyptian family. She converted the emperor's wife and many pagan philosophers to Christianity but was tortured on a wheel and eventually beheaded. Another popular saint, Barbara, was shut up in a tower by her father but miraculously escaped and was carried to the mountains, although she was finally killed by her father. Saint Paraskevi was born on a Friday and named after that day.

Saints George and Theodore

Particularly popular in Cappadocia are the Saints George and Theodore, who appear mounted on horses, often George on a white one and Theodore on a black, facing each other and together fighting a dragon at their feet. With so much military activity in Cappadocia it is not surprising that soldier heroes would be popular.

Saint Hieron

Many of the saints depicted in Cappadocian churches are the same as found elsewhere in the Byzantine world. There are however some who are distinctly local. One is Saint Hieron, a farmer from Tyana in Cappadocia who was renowned for his strength. He refused to go into the army as he knew he would be forced to worship pagan gods. Later he confessed his faith and was beheaded in Armenia. He is depicted in Tokalı kilise.

Yılanlı kilise (Snake church)

This is a primitive building with an irregular form and large simple paintings depicting favourite saints. The main nave is barrel vaulted and is entered from the north so the apse is to the left on the east side. The walls are marked out as if made of stone and therefore suggest a built church, perhaps implying that the simple chapel is grander than it really is. On the east side of the vault is Saint Onesimos (a first-century slave who converted to Christianity and was martyred), looking young and holding a white cross, with Saints George and Theodore mounted on a white and a brown horse and fighting a dragon at their feet (this looks like a snake and gives name to the church). There is also a portrait of Helena, the mother of Constantine with her son, both dressed in imperial costume and standing holding a cross between them (she is on the left and he on the right), (see box, page 19). On the other side of the vault are Saints Onouphrios (an Egyptian hermit saint), Thomas and Basil. Thomas appears as a young man, and Basil wears a Bishop's dress and holds a Gospel book.

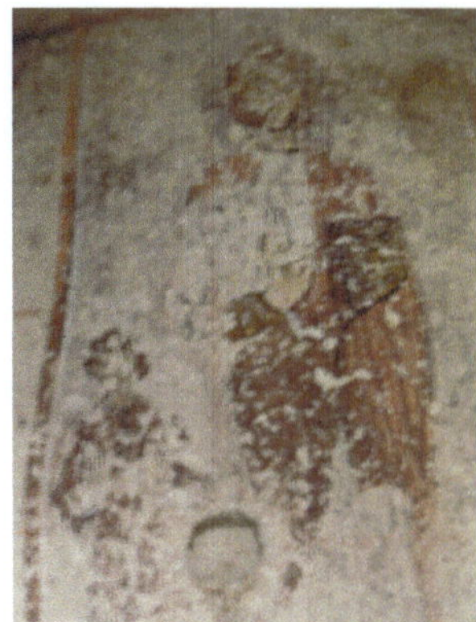

Christ and a young boy named Theodore, Yılanlı kilise, Göreme

At the far end on the south wall in **Yılanlı kilise** is a standing figure of Christ with a small young donor named Theodore at his side.

On the adjacent wall is a painting of Onouphrios, an old man with a long white beard but also with breasts. Local tradition held that **Onouphrios** was a beautiful girl who sought the attention of men. When she repented she begged God to preserve her from lust and his solution was to turn her into an old man.

St Basil

Entering this church, go through a doorway on the left into a barrel vaulted space with a portrait of Saint Basil on the immediate left. There are also portraits of Saints George and Theodore riding horses. There are apses facing to the west. The main one has an image of Christ and next to this are the Virgin and Child.

BEYOND THE OPEN AIR MUSEUM

Saklı kilise (Hidden Church) or St John's Church

This is not always open but is situated to the right of the road from Göreme to the open air museum, and reached on an attractive winding path. It is dated to about 1070. The plan is unusual with the space divided in two, laterally, so that one enters a horizontal space divided from the east part of the building by three arches supported on two piers. The Annunciation is depicted on the spandrels flanking the central arch with Saints Constantine and Helena on the soffits, the underside of the arches. On the west wall , to the right (north side) is the *Koimisis* with the Nativity on the north wall and the Baptism on the east part of the north wall beyond the arcade. Standing again at the door, to the left (south side) is the Transfiguration with the Crucifixion on the south wall. In the Crucifixion Christ's body is highlighted with stylised musculature and on either side stand the Virgin and Saint John as well as Longinus piercing Christ's side and Esopos handing him vinegar on a sponge.

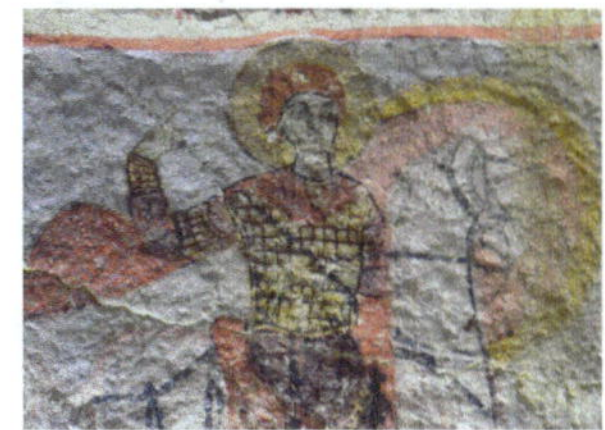

Saint George, St Basil kilise, Göreme

Saklı kilise church is distinguished by unusual and imaginative paintings probably made by local artists who drew on the familiar landscape for inspiration, depicting birds and other natural features. The scenes are simply portrayed with little background or setting.

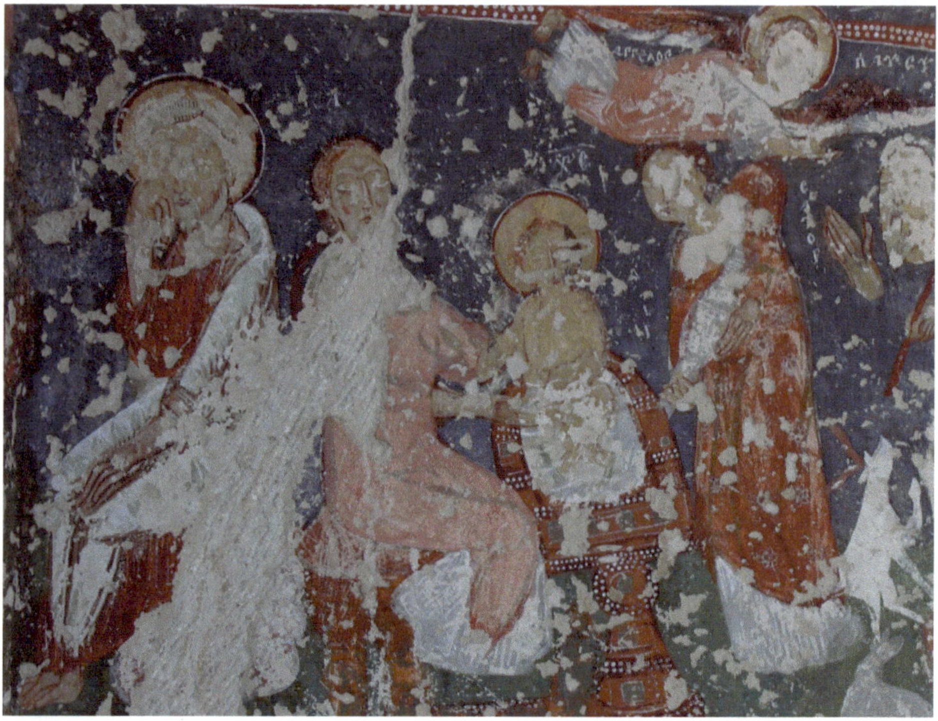

The midwives wash the Christ Child, Nativity, El Nazar kilise, Göreme

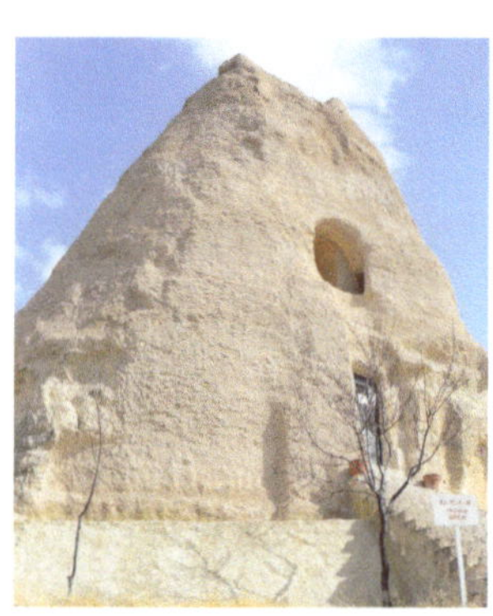

El Nazar kilise, Göreme

In **El Nazar kilise,** the background is painted in dark blue, and the colours used tend to choral red and light green with many white highlights creating patterns over the fabrics. The faces are long, pale and serious.

El Nazar kilise (Evil Eye Church)

Situated to the right of the road from Göreme to the open air museum, on a path which runs just east of the river bed, this church was excavated within an isolated cone and stands out against the skyline. It has been renovated and partially rebuilt. It is ticketed and generally open, and it is possible to drive up to the church.

The design is cross shaped, with the east part of the cross made into a horseshoe shaped apse and with a small chapel cut from the south arm of the cross.

The painting is dated to the end of the tenth century. The scene in the dome shows the Ascension. The image in the apse is a seated Virgin on a lyre backed throne and flanked by archangels. The Nativity in the vault of the south cross arm is particularly striking with Christ being bathed by two midwives in a splendid jewelled bath looking like a font. In the same vault are the Annunciation and other scenes associated with Christ's birth. The Baptism is in the west barrel vault adjacent to the door and scenes of the Passion in the north barrel vault.

Kılıçlar kilise (Sword Church)

This church has fine paintings. There are signs to it in the centre of Göreme. Situated some distance from the road, it is a cross-in-square design with a narthex with a dome over it. The decoration has an extensive programme of scenes from Christ's life culminating in the Ascension in the dome. Christ in Majesty is in the main apse and the Virgin and Child in the north apse. The date is uncertain as the painting style seems quite early, perhaps rather similar to the paintings in the Old Church at Tokalı. The architectural design of the church was used in Cappadocia in the tenth century. It has been suggested to be as early as 905 but it is perhaps more likely to be later in the century.

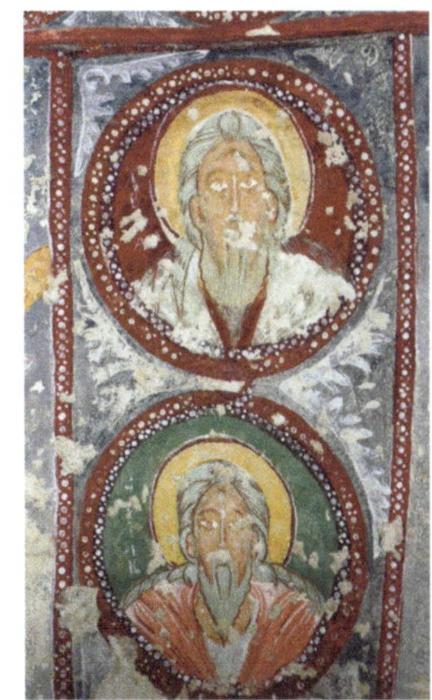

Busts of prophets, El Nazar kilise, Göreme

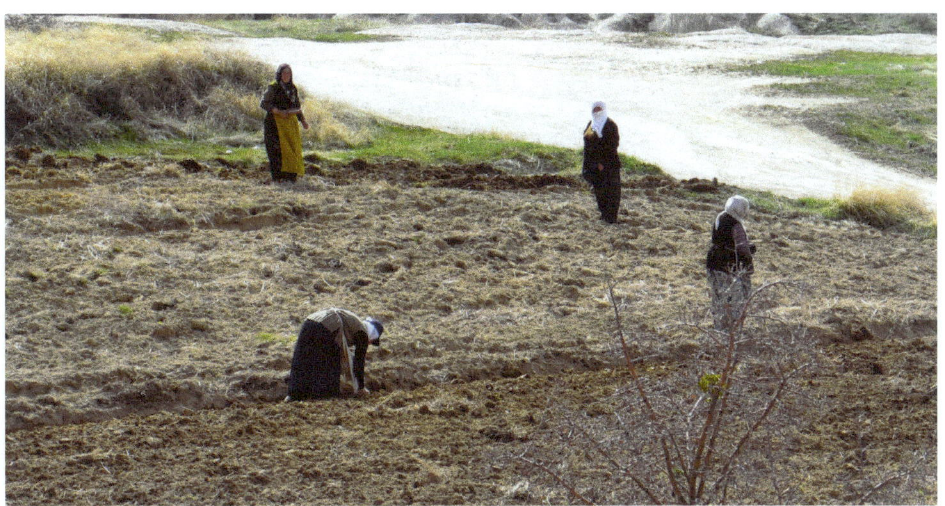

Women working in the fields by El Nazar kilise

Constantine and Helena

In many churches Helena and Constantine are depicted standing frontally together with a cross between them, dressed in imperial regalia. Helena, Constantine's mother, was held by tradition to have found the true cross on which Christ was crucified in Jerusalem, and Constantine as emperor legalised Christianity and built the first large basilical churches in Rome. They are therefore seen as saints and revered as great pillars of Christianity.

Architecture

The churches in Cappadocia largely fall into four designs: single nave, triple aisle, transverse vault and cross-in-square or quincunx. Although carved out of rock they are made to look like built churches. One joy of excavating a space is that the roof is generally self-suspending so the builder avoids the problem of how to span spaces or prop up the roof. Most of the churches are situated so the apse is in the east and many have an entryway or narthex in the west, which is usually the location of the main door. The natural form of the rock sometimes dictates the shape of the church. Many churches were used by the local people and were part of family estates or villages. Several have lower chapels or caves created for various functions.

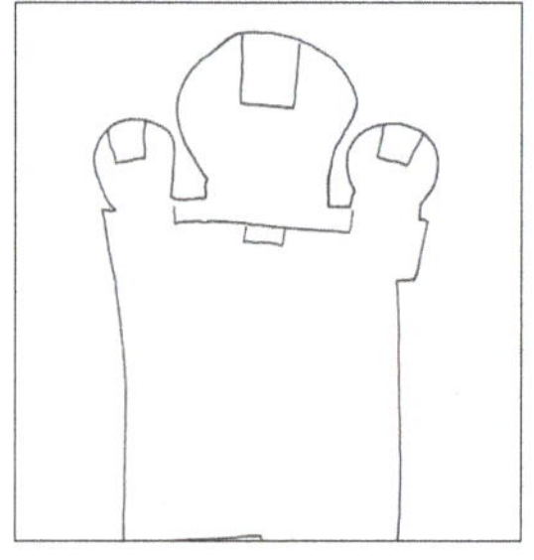

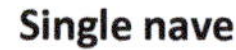

Single nave

Single nave churches have one longitudinal space which usually ends in single apse with a broad conch. Often, a barrel vault creates a rounded ceiling or, occasionally, the ceiling is flat. Occasionally this form culminates in a triple apse, as at the Church of Nikephoros Phokas in Çavuşin (page 23). A further variation is two single nave churches placed next to each other, often with a linking passage as at Ayvali (page 24).

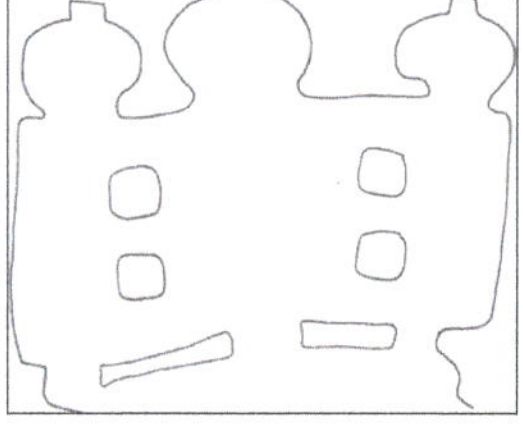

Three aisled

A similar but more complex form is the three aisled church with a central nave flanked by an aisle on each side often with an arcade dividing the aisles running from east to west. A later variation is for each aisle to culminate in an apse, giving three apses, a feature which seems to have developed for liturgical reasons in the eighth century.

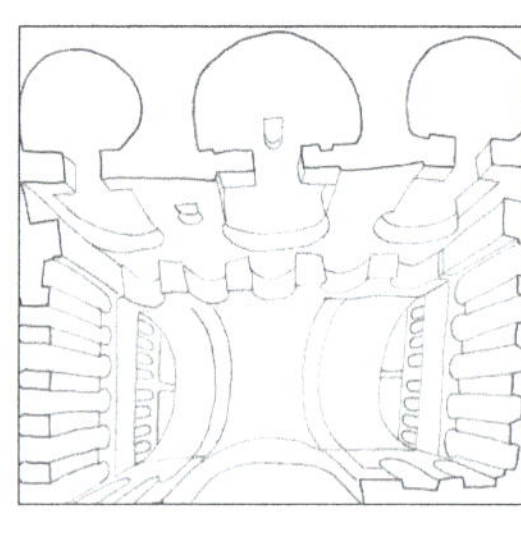

Transverse vault

An unusual church design alters the longitudinal plan to a horizontal one with a transverse barrel vault covering the main space. The focus is still on the east end, which has three apses. This is found at the New Church at Tokalı (page 10).

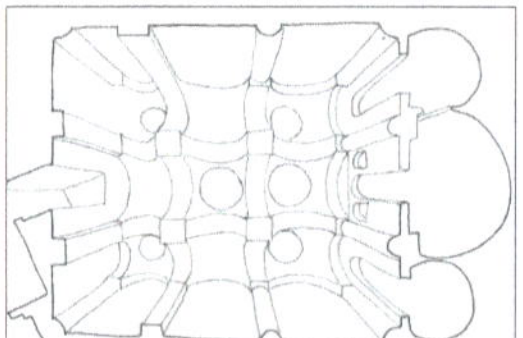

Cross-in-square

The cross-in-square plan became popular in the late ninth century and became the standard form of Byzantine church. It is particularly suited to small spaces. The basic building shape is a short rectangle (nearly square), with three apses. The central square of space is divided into nine bays, like a noughts and crosses grid. The centre bay has a four columns, one at each corner, which support the central dome on pendentives. There are usually barrel vaults in the centre bays on each side and domes in the corner bays. Sometimes the bay adjacent to the apse is also domed. The centre bays on each side thus create a cross shape within the square and have five or sometimes six domes.

CHAPTER THREE:

ÇAVUŞIN AND GÜLLÜ DERE

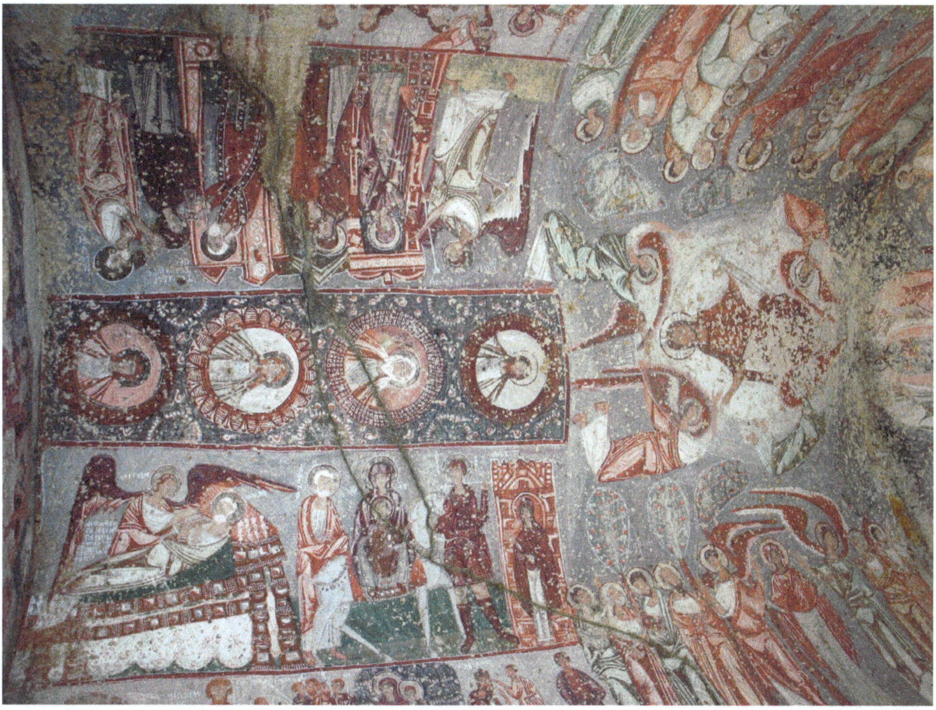

The ceiling vault, Church of Nikephoros Phokas, Çavuşin

ÇAVUŞIN

The old village of Çavuşin had to be abandoned following an earthquake in 1939 and is now an attractive hillside ruin with a combination of caves and constructed dwellings, many with decorative carvings. It is possible to climb up starting from the cafés at the bottom of the hill and then skirting the hillside to arrive at the church of St John which is high up in an excavated cave. Close to the main road, on the other side of the new village is the Church of Nikephoros Phokas, often known as the Pigeon House, which is easily accessible. Near the old village is a dirt road giving access to two beautiful and interesting valleys, Güllü dere (Rose valley) and Kızıl çukur (Red valley), which each have several churches, reachable on foot along very arresting paths. Covered here are the churches of Uç and Ayvali in Güllü dere.

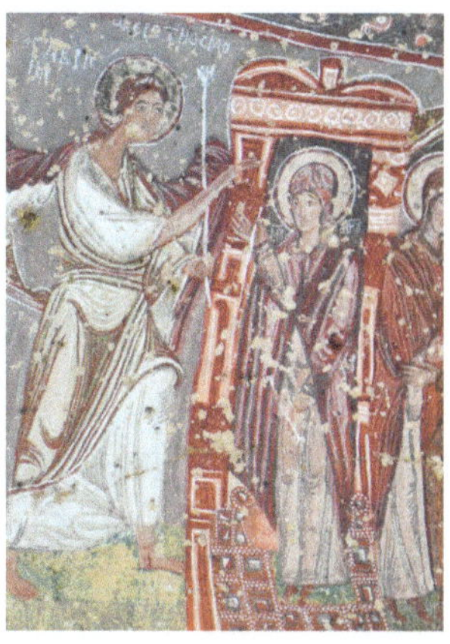

The Annunciation, Church of Nikephoros Phokas, Çavuşin

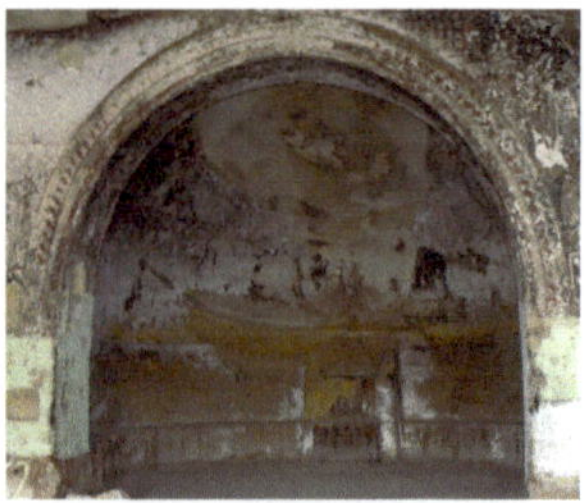

Synthronon within apse, St John the Baptist, Çavuşin

There is a bench, known as a **synthronon,** running around the lower edge of the apse, which was used by the clergy during the service, with a large seat or cathedra in the centre for the bishop. This form is common in early churches. Above the seat is a sculpted cross set within a circle. A fragmentary inscription which gives the dedication of the church to John the Baptist runs around the apse.

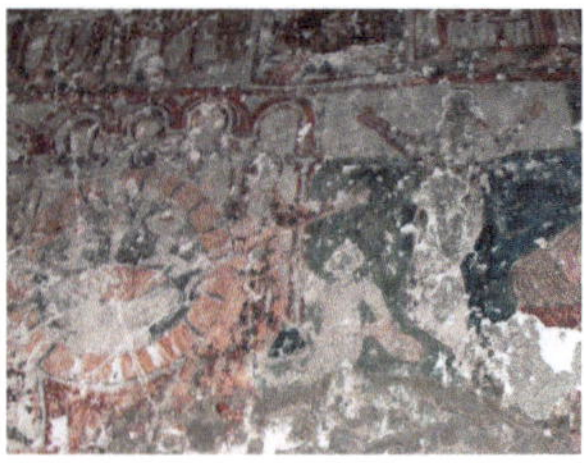

The Dance of Salome, St John the Baptist, Çavuşin

In the register over the door in the south wall is the **Feast of Herod**, with Herod and five guests seated around a circular table, to the right of which Salome dances with raised hands holding castanets. Further to the right is the headless figure of John and two servants holding his head on a platter.

In the register above, is the **Incredulity of Thomas** with Christ standing in the centre holding his right arm out to Thomas who reaches forward to touch the wound.

St John the Baptist

This church is excavated in the rock high up the hillside. It is necessary to walk from the road up through the abandoned buildings of the old village. Starting by the small shops at the right side of the rock facade, climb up and then skirt along the hillside to the outer face. A small bridge finally leads to the church.

This large basilical shaped church was perhaps excavated at the end of the fifth or beginning of the sixth century and has early paintings. It is well worth visiting as it has a magnificent site and its age and design makes it very unusual. It has been somewhat altered over time but gives an excellent sense of the appearance of an early church with its massive structure and plain carving.

The entrance now takes you into the south aisle which has a very distinctive geometrically-patterned carved rock face. From here you walk through a doorway into the main nave with the apse on the right.

The paintings are hard to read. The first phase of painting is in the expansive apse and probably dates from the end of the sixth or the beginning of the seventh century. The scene is Christ's Second Coming, but only fragments remain of the tetramorphs, seraphim and angels on either side and saints on the lower register. To the far left is the Baptism of Christ and to the far right the Transfiguration. Turning to the north wall, there are paintings on the area at the east end above the door to the adjacent aisle. These are in two registers with Infancy scenes in the upper register: the Annunciation, Visitation (mostly lost so only the legs are visible), Nativity to the right with, in the very far right, the small figures of the shepherds. In the lower register are scenes from the Passion, with the Betrayal (Judas's face can be seen reaching up to kiss Christ) on the left and the Judgement of Pilate on the right, with Pilate washing his hands and Christ standing on the right facing left. On the very far right is the figure of Simon the Cyrene carrying the cross. The narrative continues on the triumphal arch (the flat area forming an arch around the apse), where on the left of the apse is the Crucifixion showing Christ flanked by the Virgin and John, and to the right of the apse the *Anastasis* with the Ascension above. In the *Anastasis*, unusually, Hades is shown in the tomb at the bottom of the image. This suggests it is an early form of this scene. Christ is helping Adam and Eve on the right to rise out of death.

Originally the aisles were separated from the nave by arcades decorated with mouldings, supported on broad columns with plain capitals. These were filled in at a later time. There was originally a narthex to the west but it has fallen away leaving remnants of tombs.

Church of Nikephoros Phokas or the Pigeon House

This church is set back in the hillside. A modern shop is at the foot of steps leading up to the site. The church is ticketed. You climb steep steps into the single nave church which is spacious and decorated with scenes from Christ's life in the barrel vault. The style is distinctive and expressive with much red colouring in the figures and blue backgrounds.

The apse is recessed above a step and although most of the paint is lost, archangels survive on either side. There are also portraits of Constantine and Helena and various bishops. On the wall above the apse is the Transfiguration with two kneeling apostles on the right of Christ who is flanked by the prophets Moses and Elijah. Christ is shown in a mandorla of light.

Scenes from Christ's life begin in the centre of the vault on the south side with the Annunciation, and move towards the door (the west) with the Visitation, Testing by Water, and then onto the west wall with Joseph and the Virgin pictured after the Testing by Water (on the rights side) and then to the left the Journey to Bethlehem and the Nativity. Moving back onto the vault on the south side, below the Annunciation is the Adoration of the Magi.

The narrative picks up on the north side at the west end with the Dream of Joseph, followed by the Flight to Egypt with the Massacre of the Innocents below and beneath the Dream of Joseph, the Persecution of Elizabeth and the Murder of Zacharias. Returning to the west wall, on the right of the door is the Baptism, and to the left of the door is the *Anastasis*.

On the south wall of the nave are scenes of Christ's Ministry, starting at the west end with the Healing of the Blind, and moving to the west, the Raising of Lazarus and the Entry to Jerusalem. On the west wall to the right of the door is the Last Supper and the Betrayal (below the Nativity).

The narrative continues on the north wall with Christ before Pilate and the Crucifixion, depicted in two separate scenes, the second showing Christ after his death. The next scene is on the south wall beneath the Raising of Lazarus, and shows the Descent from the Cross, the Entombment and the Marys at the Tomb.

In the vault at the east end is a magnificent Ascension and Mission of the apostles spanning the entire vault. This is very likely modelled on the same scenes at the New Church at Tokalı kilise, as it is very similar. The quality of painting here is not so sophisticated and the style is simpler, so there is no suggestion that the artists were the same but that the artists here were inspired by the earlier painting which is of very high quality and innovational in this region. In the apex of the vault, there are four portraits of prophets in roundels, which, in order from east to west, depict Amos, Habakkuk, Jeremiah and Daniel.

The **Church of Nikephoros Phokas** takes its official name from an important portrait of the Byzantine emperor while its colloquial name, the Pigeon House, comes from its post-Byzantine use as a place to keep pigeons whose droppings provided useful manure. The painting can be dated, and so this helps with the dating of other churches in the area.

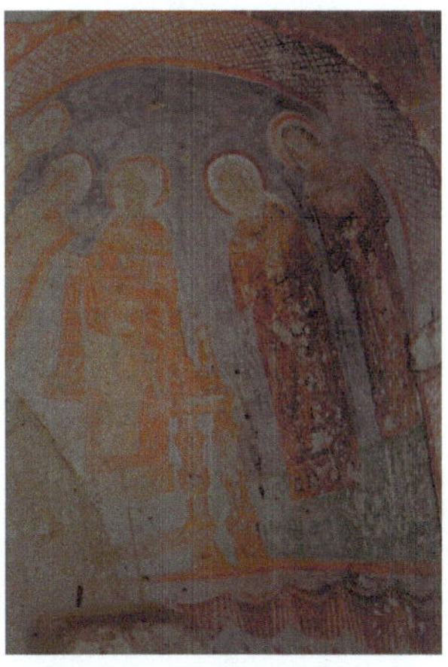

The portrait of the emperor Nikephoros Phokas and his family

The **emperor Nikephoros** stands in the centre in front of a jewelled throne, crowned and wearing imperial dress. He extends his right hand towards Theophanu, his wife, who stands to the left, also crowned. To the right of Nikephoros is his father, Bardas Phokas, and on the far right, Leo, Bardas's other son. To the far left is a further figure, perhaps the wife of Leo. Nikephoros was aged about 52 at this time and his father over 80. The inscription above Nikephoros's head reads 'Lord protect our pious emperors always, Nikephoros and our empress Theophanu'. This is the only imperial image from this time surviving outside of Constantinople.

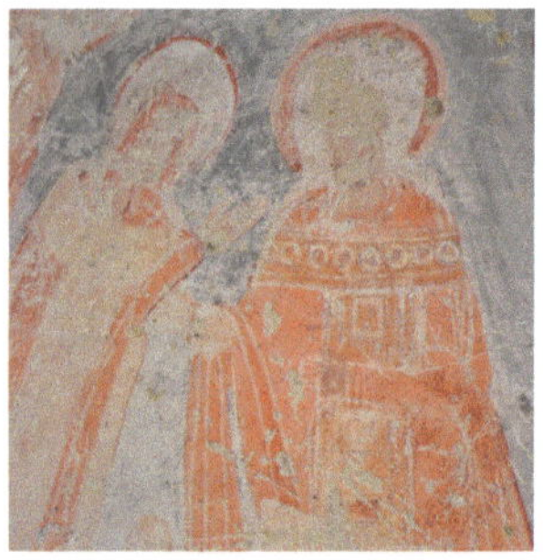

The emperor and his wife Theophanu, Church of Nikephoros Phokas, Çavuşin

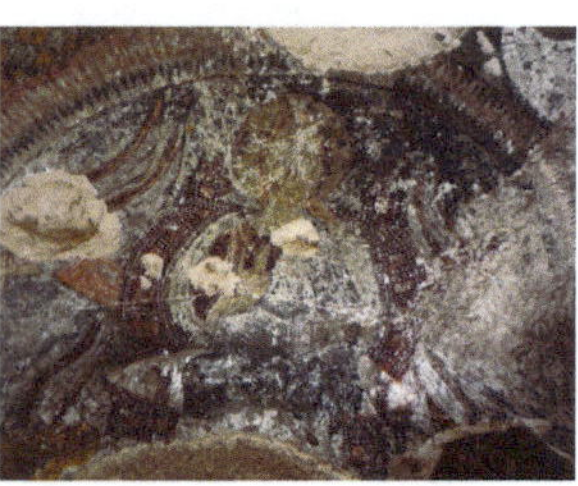

The Second Coming of Christ, ceiling of Uç kilise, Güllü dere

In the painting of the **Second Coming of Christ,** taken from the Book of Revelation, there are vivid seraphim with tetramorphs, symbols of the evangelists. These are a lion for St Mark, an ox for St Luke, an angel for St Matthew and an eagle for St John.

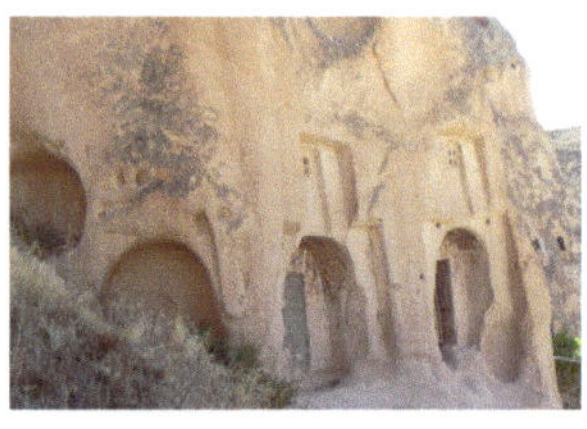

Ayvali kilise, Güllü dere

At **Ayvali kilise,** the chapels were excavated and painted in a rudimentary way and later restored by excellent artists with a sophisticated repertory of images.

The portrait of the emperor Nikephoros Phokas is in the north apse. Nikephoros came from Cappadocia and ruled from 963-69. He was himself a soldier and came from a prestigious military family. When the former emperor, Romanos II (959-63), died young leaving two small sons, Nikephoros seized power and married their mother Theophanu. He was popular because of his military achievements. The family, including the sons, accompanied him on journeys to Cappadocia between 964 and 965, where they stayed while he went to battle. It is at this time that the portrait may well have been painted. He was murdered in 969, apparently with Theophanu's approval.

GÜLLÜ DERE

This valley is signposted from the centre of Çavuşin village.

Uç kilise

The first church you come to is Uç kilise. There is a sign and looking up you can see the church is cut into the rock to the left of the path. It is a steep climb up with some narrow passages. The church has some painting but also magnificent carving in the roof showing a cross contained within a circle with four smaller circles set within it, flanked by two large abstract standing crosses with entwined rope patterns surmounted by a semicircle, each with two trees below. It is probably dated to the second half of the tenth century. The painting depicts the Second Coming of Christ or *Parousia* in the vault of the large rounded apse, flanked by the archangels Michael and Gabriel. On the wall adjacent to the apse is a scene of the Baptism.

Ayvali kilise (Church of St John)

Continuing along the arroyo, there are signs to Ayvali kilise. This church is open at times and the key holder is subject to change. Enquire at the village to find out who can give you access. This is an important church as it is both early and dateable. It has many paintings, although they are quite difficult to decipher.

Ayvali kilise consists of two single nave chapels, lying parallel to each other and connected by a passage at the east end. The west door of the northern chapel has been blocked up, and it therefore has no external door and is very dark. Each has an apse and niches in the walls. They both seem to have been excavated at the same time as their shape and size is identical; however they appear to have different functions. The south chapel has the typical series of images about Christ's life, and the north is concerned with life after death and therefore was probably intended as a burial chapel.

In the apse, Christ appears in majesty accompanied by the prophets Isaiah and Ezekiel with bishops below. The figures have an extraordinary energy and dynamism. The Lamb of God and six prophets are depicted on the soffit of the arch. Above, in the lunette, is a seated Virgin and Child with angels. In the vault at the west end spreads a large Ascension. The scenes from the life of Christ begin in the north vault at the east end with depictions of the Annunciation and then move across to the south vault with the Journey to Bethlehem and the Nativity and back to the north vault, lower register, for the Adoration of the Magi, Dream of Joseph and Flight to Egypt. They then take up across on the south vault, lower register, with the Massacre of the Innocents and the Presentation in the Temple. The story starts again at the east end of the south wall with the Baptism and then on to the Passion with the Raising of Lazarus, the Entry into Jerusalem and the Washing of the Disciples' Feet. The subsequent scenes up to the *Anastasis* are on the west and north walls, and the Transfiguration is on the west lunette. Saints are depicted on the walls.

The iconography in the north chapel concerns the Second Coming, with Christ shown at the west end in a mandorla of light with the twelve apostles, and two angels bearing a cross appear at the east end. In the apse is a *deisis* with Christ in the centre flanked by the Virgin and John the Baptist, with saints on the walls and again prophets in medallions on the arch. A further scene associated with death is the Dormition of the Virgin, depicted at the west end of the north wall.

In the south chapel at **Ayvali kilise**, if you look closely at the north wall (on the right as you enter) and up into the barrel vault, you can see traces of the **first layer of paint.** The forms are quite simple, whereas the painting of the second layer is of high quality and, due to its similar iconography and style, was surely done by the same artists as the Old Church at Tokalı kilise (page 7).

Passing into the north chapel, on the passage vault are **Elijah** with his chariot and **Elisha** receiving his mantle and on the west wall the Sacrifice of Abraham.

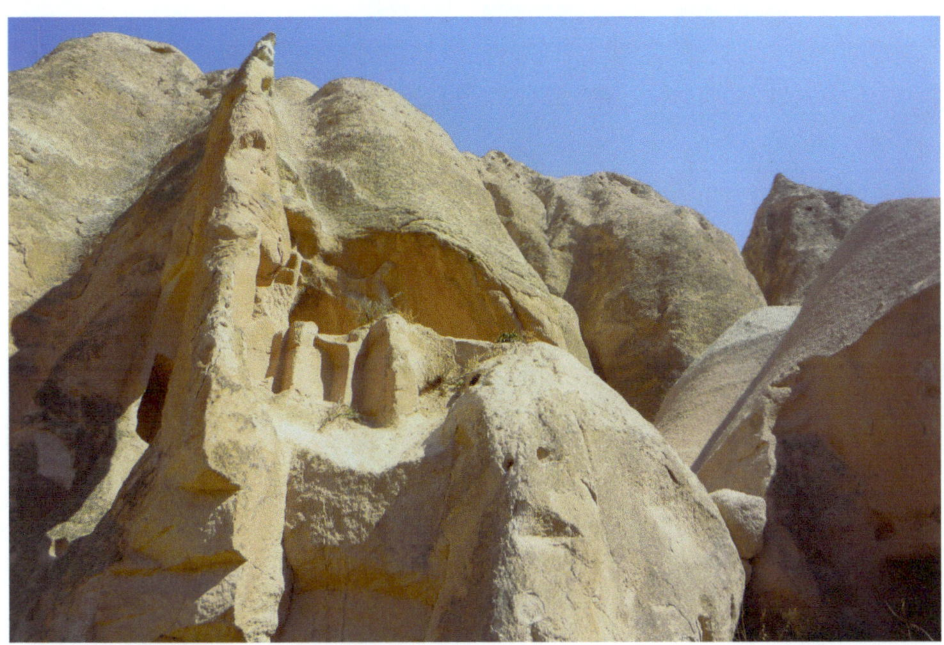

Güllü dere near Çavuşin

Monasteries

Some of the churches were attached to monasteries. These were religious communities established for a very small group, perhaps originating with one hermit to whom others were drawn, as seems to be the case at Karabaş Kilise in the Soğanlı valley, where the monks are pictured (page 29). It is thought that few of the Cappadocian monasteries housed more than twenty or so monks or nuns.

The tradition of monasticism originated in Egypt in the third century. Saint Anthony lived as a hermit in seclusion and other hermits were drawn towards his ascetic zeal. This is known as eremitic monasticism. In the fourth century, monks began to live together in communities, known as cenobitic monasticism. Basil the Great, a wealthy aristocrat from Cappadocia who became bishop of Caesarea, articulated a series of aspirations and perameters known as the 'Rule of Basil', which became the foundation for monastic communities.

The monasteries must have been integrated to a certain extent with the local communities and often the donors depicted in the paintings at monastic churches are laymen and women, such as at Karabaş Kilise where Michael Skepides, Protospatharios, a high court dignitary who was perhaps a local governor, is named and pictured as a patron.

There were also groups of women living together in nunneries. At Karabaş kilise again, one of the donors is named as a nun and she also is pictured in the church wearing her nun's dress. It was fairly common for both men and women to retire to a monastery at some point in their lives, either when getting old, or having lost political favour, or when widowed. Byzantine aristocrats might give money to an already established monastery or found one themselves and so create a place they might retire to in relative comfort and security.

It is not always clear in Cappadocia which churches are associated with monasteries and which were made for worship by lay communities. These may have been fairly well integrated so that local people participated in the monastic churches.

In many Cappadocian churches, the paintings have been altered by **graffiti,** written in Greek, Turkish and other languages, and some of the faces and figures have been defaced, with the eyes in particular being damaged.

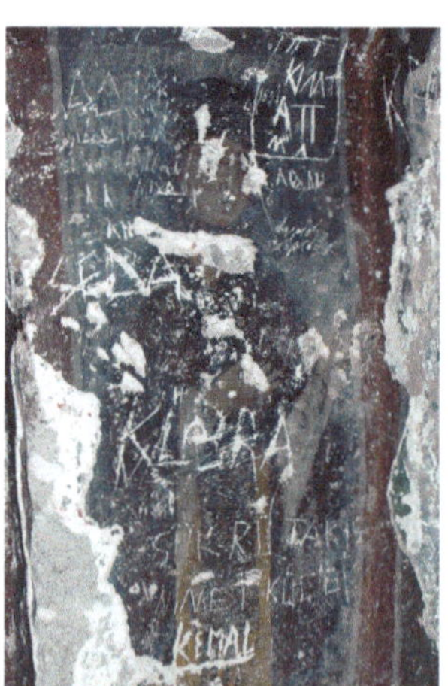

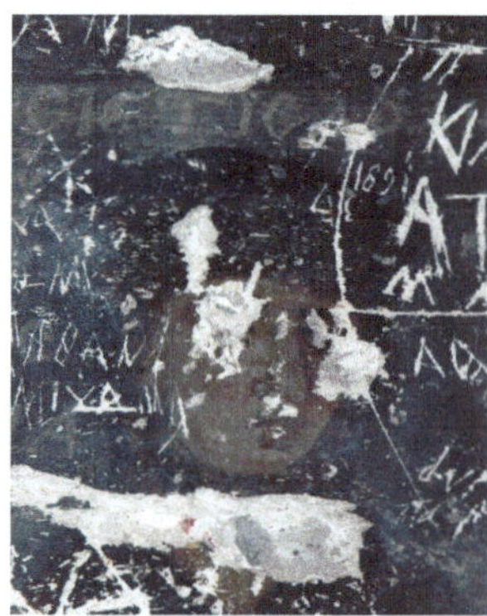

Full length and detail of female nun donor at Karabaş, kilise in the Soğanlı Valley

CHAPTER FOUR

THE SOĞANLĪ VALLEY

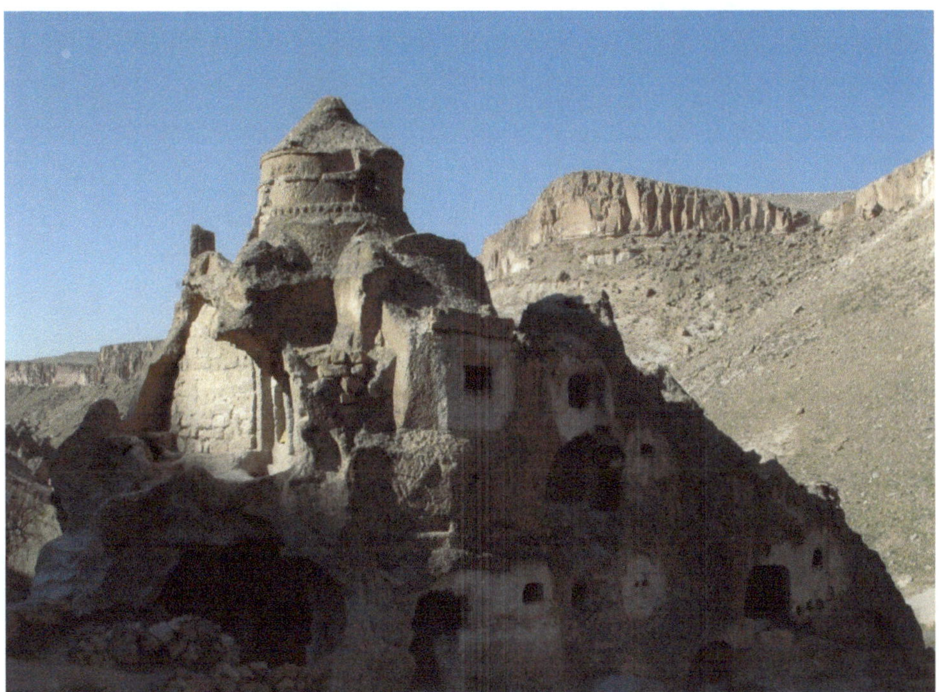

Kubbeli kilise, Soğanlı valley

The Soğanlı valley is a spectacular spot about 60 kms and an easy drive to the south of Göreme. There is a nominal fee to enter the valley area in which there are several churches, many of which are within reasonable walking distance. The churches are marked with signs. They are arranged here according to the most obvious route. Following the road to the right after passing by the ticket office, there are two churches to the right of the road, Karabaş kilise and Yılanlı kilise. After visiting these, proceed up the valley and cross the river at the bridge following the path on the other side which leads back in the direction you have just come. On the left of the path there are two churches, Kubbeli and Saklı. Retrace your steps back down to near the entrance and turn right across the road bridge and walk a little further to the bend in the river, cross the bridge and you are at St Barbara, also known as Tahtalı kilise You can also reach all these except Kubbeli and Saklı by car. A torch is needed to see the interiors.

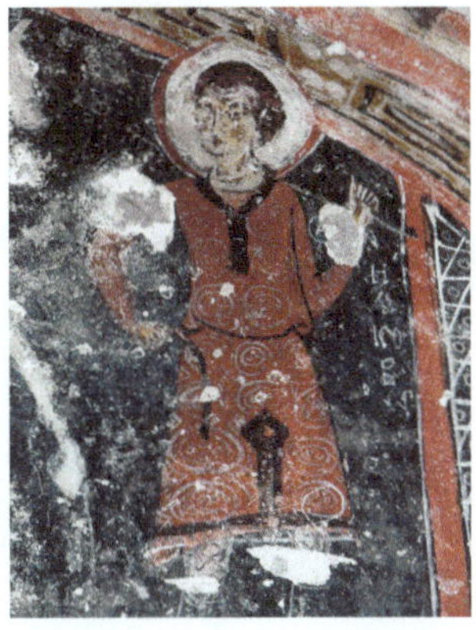

Joseph's son, Jacob, St Barbara kilise, Soğanlı valley

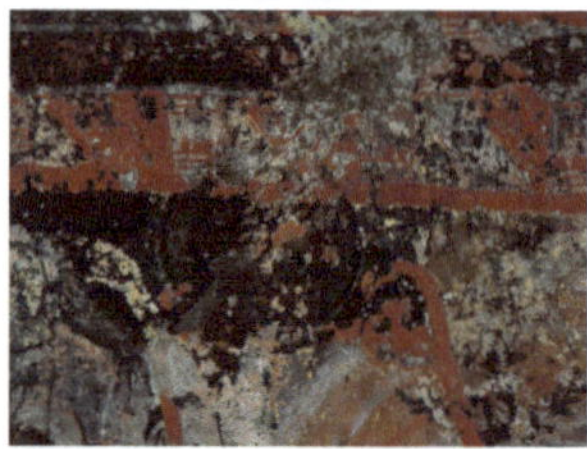

The head of an angel with an earlier layer of paint above his head, Karabaş kilise, Soğanlı valley

The first chapel at **Karabaş kilise** has been painted three times, and in places you can still see the **three layers of paint**, which are said to date to the tenth century, about 1050 and finally 1060/61. It is this third layer of paint which is most clearly visible. From the first layer is a rudimentary **portrait of a monk**. It is on the right (east) face of the first niche to the left of the entrance (the west niche on the north wall). There is an inscription saying 'Lord, help your servant, Roustiakos'. The second layer of paint shows through the top one so that it is possible to see the lines separating the registers in the barrel vault, and on the north wall parts of the top layer have fallen off revealing at least one figure.

Karabaş kilise (Black Head Church)

This is a fascinating church with several chapels and portraits of monks and donors. The paintings are dated by an inscription to 1060/61.

Climb up the hillside to the church whose entrance is through a curved porch. You enter a single nave chapel which is the first of four chapels. Adjacent to this one and parallel to it, reached through three openings in the south wall, is a slightly smaller single nave chapel. A passage from its south wall leads into a further single nave space set facing at a slight angle. A burial chamber lies down a passage from its west wall, but more intriguingly a further fourth chapel is reached either through a tunnel in the southwest corner or by clambering over the south wall which has been partially knocked down.

The second and third chapels have rudimentary painting of encircled crosses whereas the first chapel is fully painted. The top layer of paint is distinctively coloured with strong rust tones, pink and brown. The figures are graceful and expressive, with luminous faces that often turn in three quarters view, participating in the scene but giving the viewer a clear impression of their expressions. The drapery clings in emphatic circular folds to the bodies, highlighted in white, and the women's garments are often edged in white emphasising the energised movement of the fabric.

In the apse is the Communion of the Apostles, a scene in which Christ appears twice at the altar distributing communion to six apostles on each side. The Annunciation is on the east wall with Gabriel and the Virgin flanking the apse. The Nativity and Presentation are on the south vault, with the Crucifixion, Women at the Tomb and *Anastasis* on the north. The Transfiguration is on the west wall above the door. Figures of saints stand on the walls along with donors.

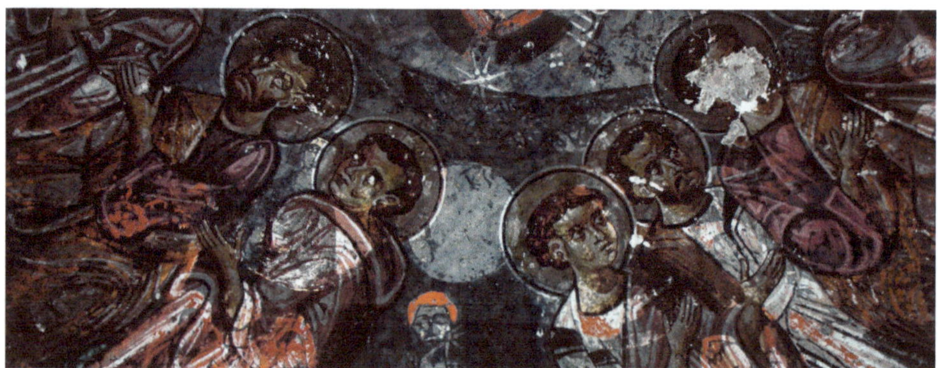

Communion of the Apostles in the apse, showing some of the apostles grouped on each side, Karabaş kilise, Soğanlı valley. The figure in the centre is from an earlier layer of paint,

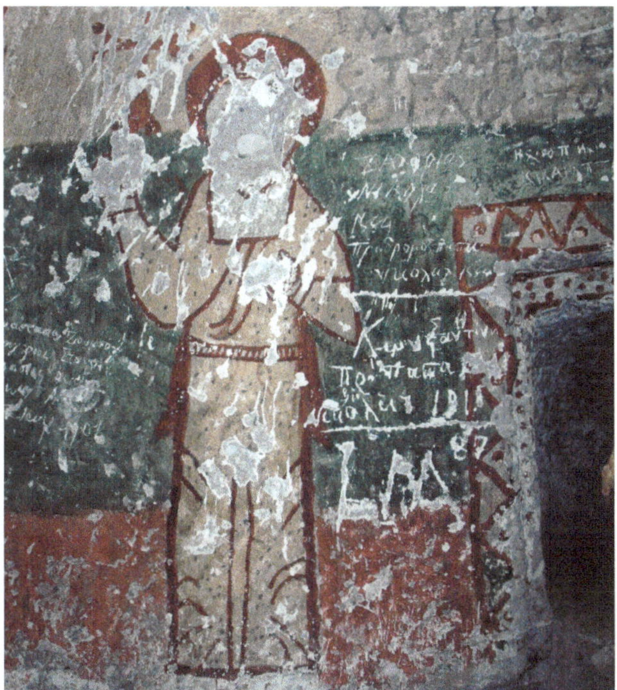

Portrait of a monk named Zacharias in the fourth chapel, Karabaş kilise, Soğanlı Valley

In the fourth chapel are paintings of the monks who prayed here and were perhaps buried in this chamber. Unfortunately two of the original four portraits were lost when the wall between this and the adjacent chapel was damaged. On the east wall, in the left corner is a monk holding a cross and wearing a habit and hat. The inscription names him as the servant of God, Zacharias, and gives the date of his death as the third of February. The two, now lost, monks looked similar and their deaths were also dated. In the right corner of the north wall is the Abbot who painted his own picture.

The inscription next to the painting of the Abbot reads 'I Bathystrokos Abbas who worked hard for this church and thereafter died, lie here. I died in the month...'. Clearly no one thought or was able to fill in the date of his death. He wears a blue *omophorion* and a pointed hood. Presumably he also painted the portraits of his colleagues.

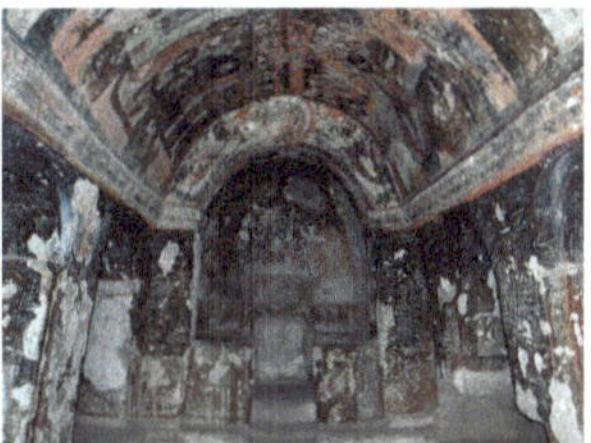

Karabaş kilise, facing west, Soğanlı valley

An inscription on the west wall tells that the decoration was paid for by Michael Skepides, Protospatharios, by the nun Catherine and by the monk Nyphon in the year 1060/61. There is an injunction that states, 'you who read this, pray for them, through the Lord. Amen'. Michael is shown in a portrait on the east facing wall in the east arch of the south wall (facing the apse, on your right, the arch nearest the apse, on the wall facing the apse). Catherine is also painted on the east facing reveal of the west niche on the north wall (facing the apse, in the niche furthest from the apse on the left, on the reveal that faces the apse). On the back wall of the centre niche on the north wall (the one to the right of the niche with Catherine), is a portrait, probably, of Nyphon who appears with a woman, Eudokia, who is perhaps his wife. They are kneeling at the feet of the Archangel Michael. It was common in Byzantine society for married people to retire to a monastery or nunnery although, rather oddly, in this portrait Nyphon is in secular not religious dress.

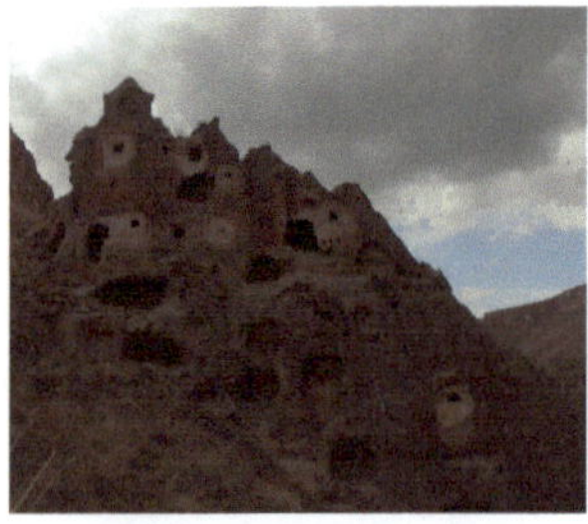

Kubbeli kilise, Soğanlı valley

Unusually, and most beautifully, the exterior of **Kubbeli kilise** is sculpted to create a small tower with a conical dome.

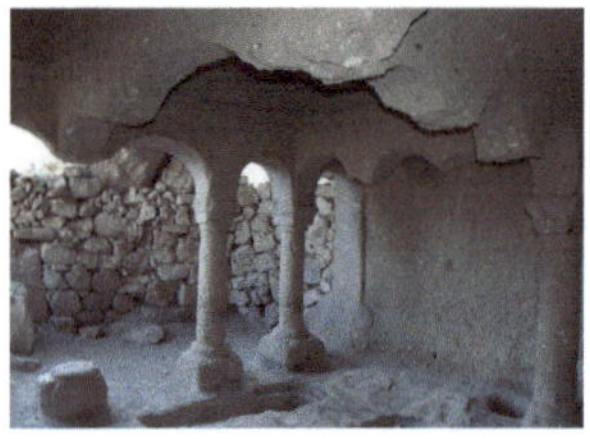

The lower church at Kubbeli kilise, Soğanlı valley

The lower church at **Kubbeli kilise** is unpainted which gives it a beautiful simplicity and highlights the design with its partially broken arcade running around the sides of the chamber and dentil cornice on the walls.

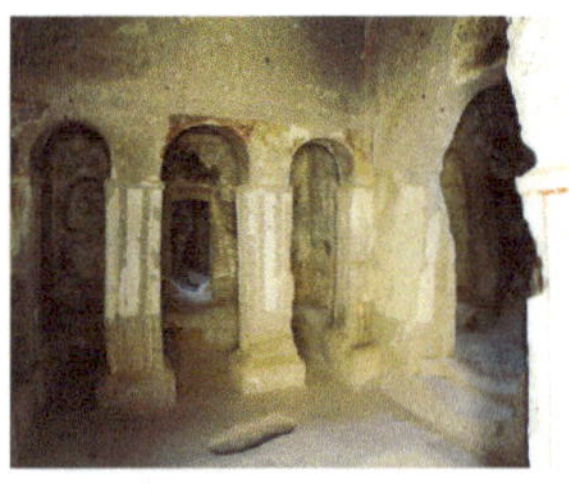

The lower church at Saklı kilise, Soğanlı valley

In the lower church at **Saklı kilise** the pilasters have been sculpted with vertical ribs and then plastered.

Yılanlı kilise (Church of the Snake)

This is a very dark church with some fairly late paintings with large images including Judgement Day and the Massacre of the Innocents.

Crossing over the small river, come back on the other side of the valley. The path shortly arrives at two churches.

Kubbeli kilise (Dome church)

This is a double church with an upper and a lower chapel, with additional spaces below. The upper church is painted although not now in good condition. Christ is in the apex of the central dome with a patterned border around the lower rim. The paint throughout is fragmentary but rust and greens predominate, with several large standing saints and scenes from the life of Christ.

Saklı kilise (Hidden church)

This is again a double church with wonderful views over the valley. It is dated to the end of the tenth century. It has a porch with an arcade. The lower church is painted but the condition is poor and the paintings are hard to decipher. It has piers with fluted carving. The main church was designed as a triple nave church with arcades and three apses.

The painting that survives is mostly in the vaults, with various saints and apostles in the south nave and scenes from Christ's life in the central and north ones. Beginning in the central nave at the east end, south part of the vault, there is the Annunciation, Visitation and Testing by Water, with the Nativity over the west door and the Adoration of the Magi and Flight to Egypt on the north part of the vault. Returning to the south vault, lower register, the narrative continues with the Massacre of the Innocents and the Persecution of Elizabeth, and, back to the north, lower register, the Presentation in the Temple and the Murder of Zacharias. Continuing in the south nave, the story picks up with John the Baptist at the east end of the vault, and, moving westwards, the Preaching of John and Christ with John. The *Anastasis* is on the west wall of the central nave.

There is even a further part of the structure below the lower church but this is hard to get to.

Tahtalı kilise (St Barbara)

This church is of interest as it is dateable to either 1006 or 1021, so some forty or sixty years before the redecoration of Karabaş kilise nearby. It has a single nave and barrel vault. A smaller space to the north appears to be a burial chapel and was built later as the wall of the larger space is broken through to access it.

An arched recess in the south wall of the church contains a child-size grave. The iconography of the painting is suited to

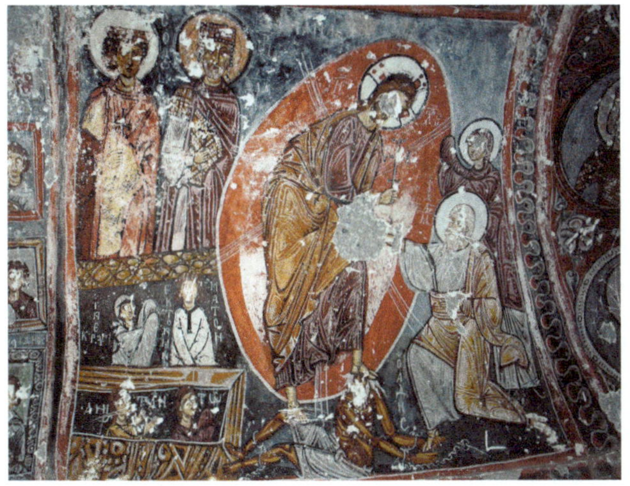

The *Anastasis*, Barbara kilise, Soğanlı valley

In **Barbara kilise**, the **inscription naming the patron** is on the west wall of the church above the entrance. It records that the church, dedicated to St Barbara, was decorated on May 5th in the year 65, indiction four, under the emperors Basil II and Constantine VIII by Basileios, the *domestikos*. The only fourth indictions in the reigns of these emperors were in 1006 and 1021 (indictions ran in 15 year cycles, so each year was named from one to fifteen). Basileios's title is slightly unclear and he may have been either a clerical or a military *domestikos*, but the latter seems more likely.

the idea of death and resurrection, so the building of the church may have been specifically to mark a child's death. The *Anastasis* in the barrel vault, depicts Christ reaching to the right to raise Adam and Eve out of Hades, while on the left, Kings David and Solomon are depicted in imperial dress.

In the apse, Christ is enthroned in a large roundel of light surrounded by the four symbols of the evangelists (an angel for Matthew, a lion for Mark, an ox for Luke and an eagle for John), as if in the Second Coming, with Adam and Eve bowed down in each corner. With the *Anastasis* in the barrel vault are the usual scenes concerning the birth of Christ.

The *Deisis* on the east end of the south wall has been partially destroyed by the burial niche cut into the wall but you can still see the heads of the figures. On the north side of the west wall, there are also various saints including three female ones, Paraskevi, Catherine and Anastasia.

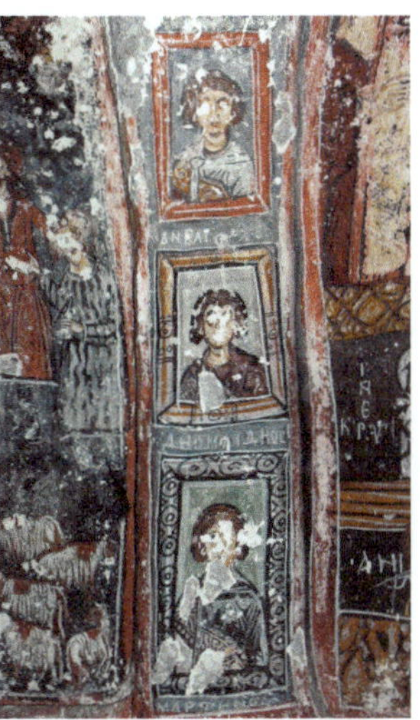

Three of the seven sleepers of Ephesus, Barbara kilise, Soğanlı valley

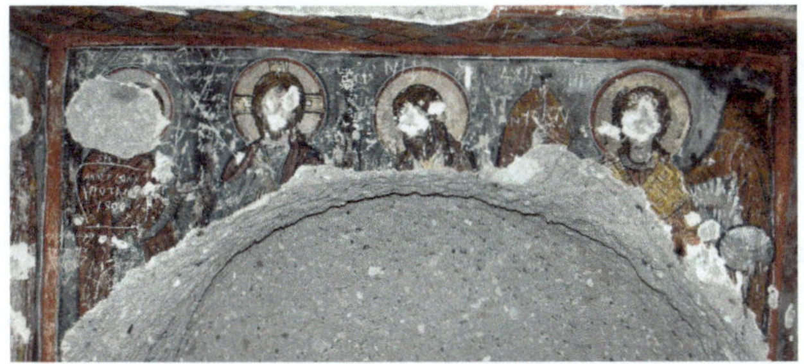

The *Deisis*, with the Virgin, Christ, John the Baptist,and an archangel, Barbara kilise, Soğanlı valley

The **seven sleepers of Ephesus** are a group of Christian youths who lived in the third century and hid in a cave to escape persecution. They awoke some two centuries later after Ephesus was Christianised. They are therefore associated with the idea of eternal life. Here they are shown as if in framed portraits arranged in a row.

Sculptured decoration

The designer of a rock cut church has the bonus of being able to create sculptural decoration as part of the excavation process. However, this is usually simple and austere. A common feature to decorate an exterior or interior wall was blind arcades, generally, in the Middle Byzantine period (9th to 12th centuries), quite elongated in shape or given horseshoe arches and occasionally surrounded by mouldings. Some of these arches have volutes where the arch springs, as on the church exterior at Eski Gümüsler, suggesting perhaps a capital (page 39). The blind arcades are excellent vessels for painted figures, as seen at Tokalı New Church (page 10). The columns and capitals were usually kept simple in form. During the Middle Byzantine period, capitals were not made in the classical Corinthian or Composite style with elements extending beyond the form of the capital, but the decoration was on the surface often with a geometrical or floral pattern. String courses, running horixontally, sometimes patterned with dentils, are often created to encircle spaces, marking off walls and bays, and walls are articulated by pilaster strips. Doors, sometimes horseshoe shaped, are decorated with various layers of mouldings and cornices. Often the sculpted surface would have been highlighted in paint, which is still visible in places. This would have drawn attention to the decoration.

Precious objects

Liturgical vessels

The churches would have contained various movable objects which are now lost or in collections, such as liturgical vessels (patens for the eucharistic bread and chalices for the wine), curtains to hang across doorways, cloths to cover the altars, candle sticks and incense burners. Depending on the wealth of the foundation, these would have been made of simple materials (ceramics for the vessels, linen for the cloths), or precious ones (silver, gold and silks).

Manuscripts

Perhaps the most prized things in churches were the manuscripts and icons. Some manuscripts that have survived are thought to have been made in Cappadocia, probably in the larger centres. Various manuscripts were used, Gospels and Old Testaments, Psalters and Lectionaries (in which the readings are arranged as they are used in the liturgical calendar). The most luxurious of these would have been illustrated. They were made from parchment and written and decorated by hand, sometimes by monks, sometimes by professional scribes.

Icons

Icons were an important element in religious practice from early times. The term icon derives from the Greek *eikon*, meaning image, and can refer to any pictorial representation, but is currently used to refer to a portable wooden panel. Early icons are made from encaustic, a wax substance, painted on a wooden panel usually prepared with linen and gesso. Tempera, pigment suspended in egg, became more customary after the ninth century. Each church would have one or more icons, which were placed on the altars and perhaps beside doorways and in niches. They would have been appropriate to the dedication of the church or chosen by the local people to depict their favourite saints or scenes. People would kiss the icons, bow before them and address their prayers to them. Icons were sometimes carried in processions from church to church or from village to village on special feast days.

CHAPTER FIVE

THE IHLARA VALLEY

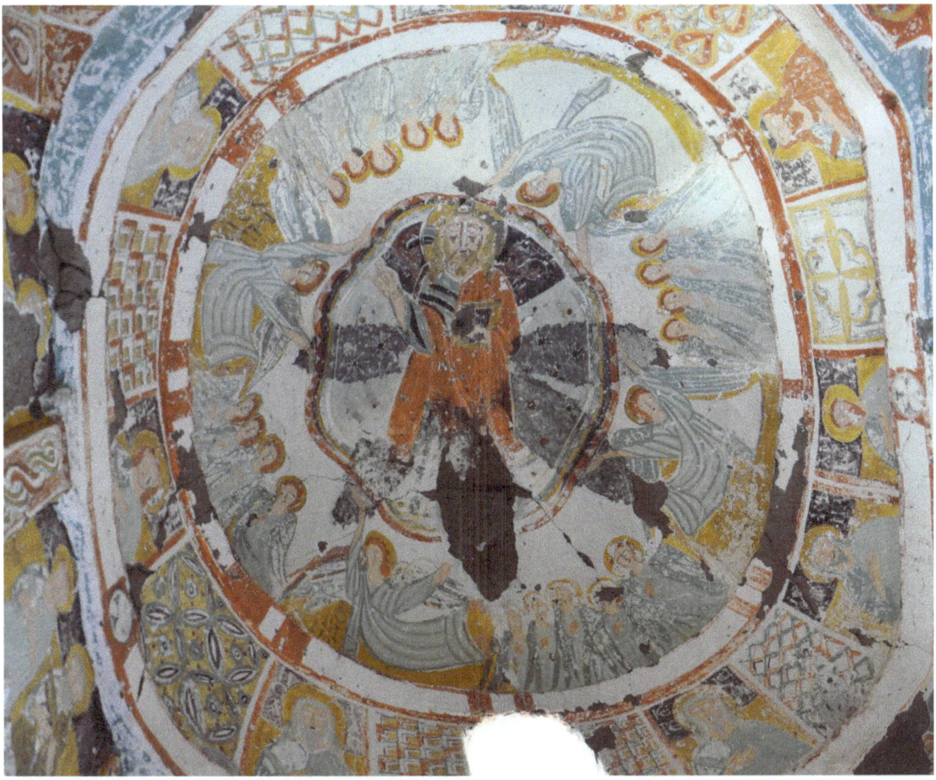

Christ in Majesty in the dome, Ağaç Altı kilise, Ihlara valley

The beautiful valley of the Melendiz River, some 90 kms southwest of Göreme, has many painted rock cut churches. Unlike the Soğanlı valley, this is lush and green, and paths on the river banks offer lovely walks between the small villages over about 12 kms. Access to the valley has a nominal fee and is at four points, Selime in the north, Belisırma, in the middle, Ihlara in the south, and between Ihlara and Belisırma where there are steps descending into the valley. The main group of churches are between Belisırma and Ihlara. Belisırma is a tranquil village by the water and good for lunch or a rest, whereas the entry by the steps is more commercial. The churches are described here as if visiting the ones at the bottom of the steps, then walking south as far as Kokar kilise then returning to the steps and north along the valley to Belisırma. Each church is signposted.

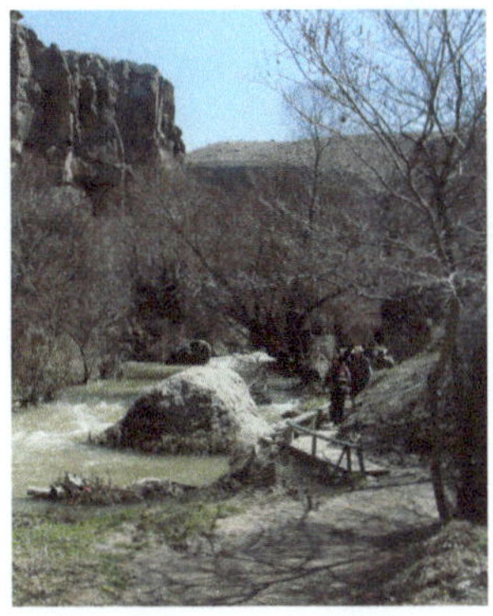

Walking in the Ihlara valley

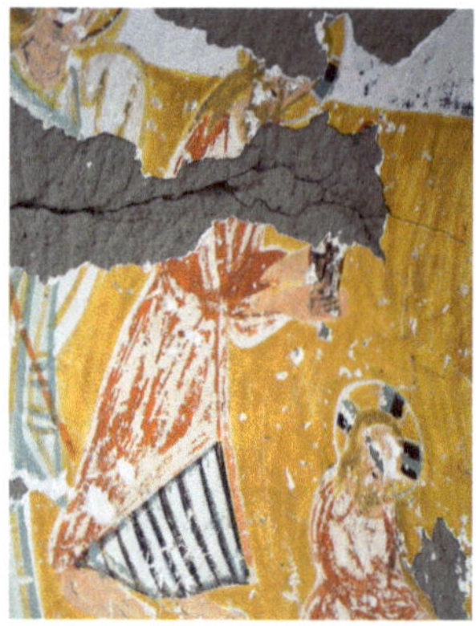

Christ in the dormition of the Virgin, Ağaç Altı kilise, Ihlara valley

Of particular interest at **Ağaç Altı kilise** is the Dormition which is shown in a very unusual way with Christ depicted twice, once at the side of his mother and again, behind, holding her soul in the form of a small child. The apostle John stands to the right and an angel in the sky to the left of Christ.

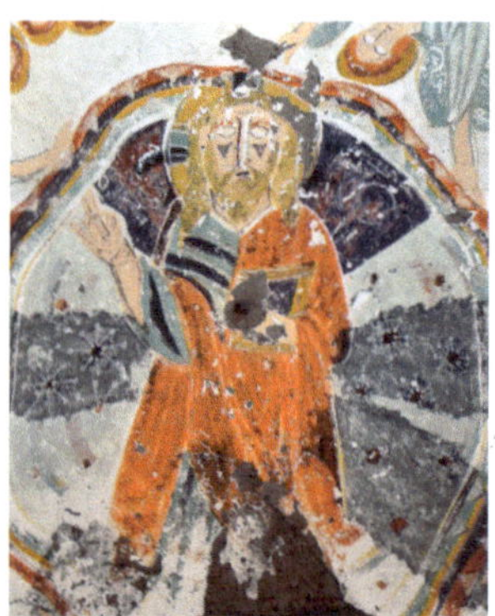

Christ in the dome, Ağaç Altı kilise, Ihlara valley

The style of the image of **Christ in the dome** is not typically Byzantine. There are several ideas about where the influence might be from, perhaps the Arab world or remnants of early Christian designs.

The first church reached descending the steps is:

Ağaç Altı kilise (Church under the Tree)

This church has a simple and beautifully coloured series of paintings. It is dated to the beginning of the eleventh century. The apse is partially lost so that you enter from the east end to stand directly beneath the central dome. This is irregular in shape and portrays Christ's Ascension with Christ in the centre supported by the four archangels and a cohort of angels with a row of prophets in square frames below. The dome is supported on squinches between which the apostles are painted as if standing between pilasters decorated with swirling patterns. The barrel vaulted nave lies ahead to the west and two arms forming a cross lie to north and south. The traces of an inscription can be read on the tympanum in the west (facing you as you enter), which records that the church was dedicated to the Virgin Pantanassa, Queen of All. In the south arm is the Annunciation on the east wall, the Visitation and the Nativity on the south, and the Adoration of the Magi on the west wall. In the north arm is the Flight to Egypt on the east wall, the Baptism on the north and the Dormition on the west. In the west tympanum is Daniel with the lions.

The ground of the paintings cycle is white but the background in each image is ochre, either set out as a square of rather intriguingly cut off at the head height of the figures as if representing the earth disappearing on the horizon. The other colours used are burnt red and light turquoise. This limited palette has a very simple coherent appearance. The figures are large and many are facing frontally in a frank and engaging way, as, for instance, the Virgin in the Annunciation and Joseph in the Flight to Egypt. The faces are delineated with single brown lines with no shading. The vault of the nave is decorated with aniconic patterns in the same palette, large scale and jubilant in mood.

Descending further, the second church reached is:

Sümbüllü kilise (Church of the Hyacinth)

Part of a monastery, Sümbüllü kilise is dated perhaps to the tenth or beginning of the eleventh century. It has a graceful upper facade which gives an impression of opulence. Cut into the rock above the church, the facade has a series of horseshoe shaped openings and blind windows which lead into an upper chamber (you can get up to this point by squeezing up a passageway in the interior).

The entrance leads to a barrel vaulted room which has minimal decoration, but through an opening on the left or north wall, is the small irregular church which was fully decorated with a central dome, a large central apse and two side aisles, each with an apse. Christ Pantokrator is in the dome, with saints Menas, Sergios and Bakchos adjacent in the vault. Other saints are on the walls, including Saints Barbara, Marina and Paraskevi as well as Tryphon and George. Several of the saints have their hands raised to their breasts, a sign of prayer. In the south aisle, the *Koimisis* or Dormition is in the apse. The Virgin lays on a bed with Christ standing behind her holding her soul in the form of a baby, while an angel flies in the sky to the left. The Annunciation is on the adjacent wall and Solomon in the vault.

From the bottom of the steps, you can either turn right to the south or turn left to the north, which is the most commonly taken route. If you turn to the right, Pürenlı Seki kilise and Kokar kilise are further south on the west side of the river and only discussed here briefly. There are other churches too, some on the east side of the river which can be found by following the signs.

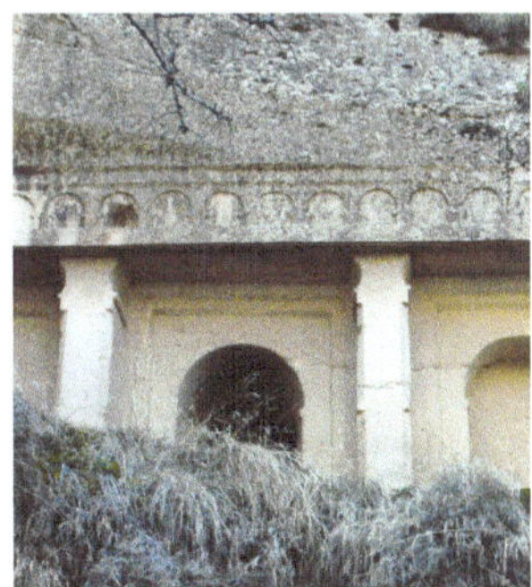

The facade of Sümbüllü kilise, Ihlara valley

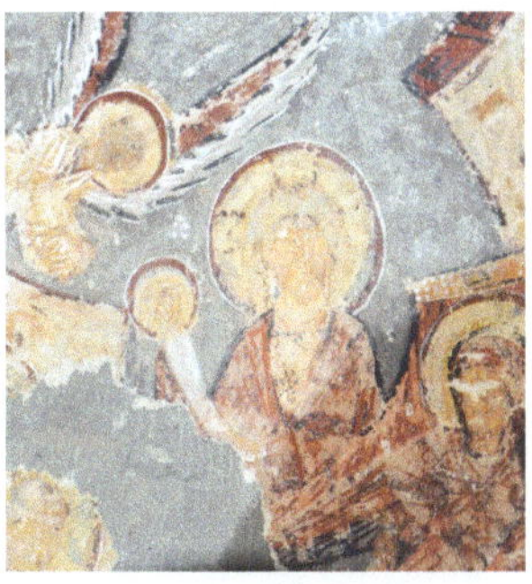

The Dormition of the Virgin, Sümbüllü kilise, Ihlara valley

The paintings at **Sümbüllü kilise** are high in quality with balance and proportion and gentle colours. The overall background is in grey with red patterned borders decorated with diamond and foliate designs. In the Dormition of the Virgin, known as the *Koimisis*, the *Theotokos* or Mother of God lies to the right on a bed. Christ stands behind her and holds his mother's soul towards the angels. The soul is in the form of a baby.

Pürenlı Seki kilise

This church is a ten minute or so walk from the steps. It is dated to the middle or second half of the eleventh century. The narthex has an adjoining burial chamber. The church has a single nave with an adjacent slightly smaller single nave chapel. The Virgin is in the apse, prophets in the apex of the barrel vault and scenes from the life of Christ in two registers below and on the west wall.

Kokar kilise

This church is dated to the second half of the twelfth century. It is entered through the now lost apse into the single nave with two burial chambers at the west end. In the vault is the Ascension and Pentecost with the apostles and scenes from the Nativity and Passion on the walls.

If you turn to the left at the bottom of the steps, walk up a little way then cross the river by the bridge then take the path on the left which winds up to Yılanlı kilise.

Yılanlı kilise (Church of the Snake)

This church is named after a rather extraordinary scene on the west wall of the narthex featuring devils in the form of snakes. You enter from the south via a small vestibule into the narthex with a dark barrel vaulted nave to your right which is fully painted. Allow your eyes to adjust to the darkness and make out the wide decorative borders that demarcate the various parts of the church including the short cross arms.

The apse is divided from the nave by the chancel screen decorated in a green and white zigzag pattern on a red ground. Above on the face of the arch are two saints, Stephen and

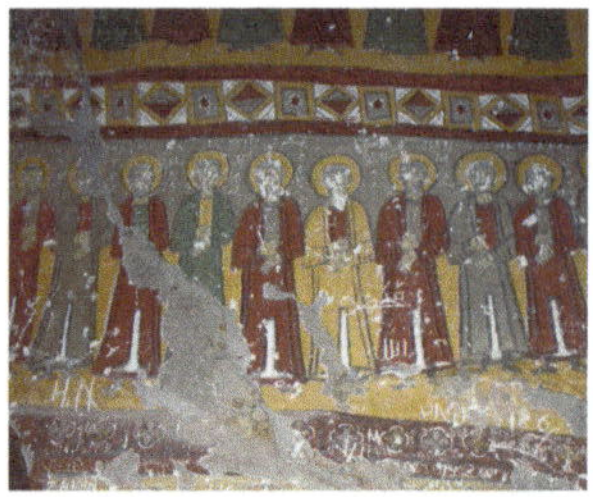

Twenty four Elders, Yılanlı kilise, Ihlara valley

Depictions of the **Last Judgement** are not common in Cappadocia, and the iconography of the twenty four elders is very unusual in Byzantine art. The elders are not normally shown in scenes of the Apocalypse although they are found in Early Christian art. The style is unusual with its rather brutal colours and lack of naturalism, quite similar to the paintings at Pürenlı Seki and Kokar churches.

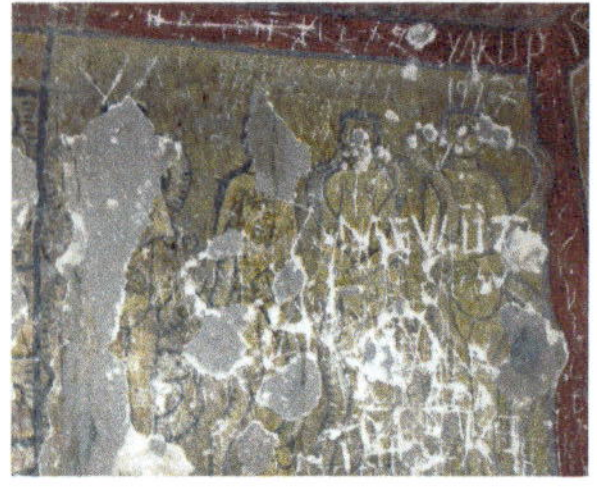

Women bitten by snakes, Yılanlı kilise, Ihlara valley

Included in the Last Judgement, is a vernacular scene. In the centre is a **three headed snake**, each head devouring a person. On the right are four women being punished by snakes. The first is bitten by eight serpents (this is largely lost), the second is bitten by a snake on her nipples as she refused to breast feed her children, the third is bitten on her mouth because she lied, and the fourth on her ears as she disobeyed.

Gamaliel (a Pharisee who defended the apostles), and an ornate border. In the apse is Christ in Majesty holding the Gospel and seated in a mandorla of light with a colourful border supported by the four floating archangels with red haloes and pink and ochre garments defined with abstract folds. Below are the Virgin and Child seated on an elaborate pearl studded, lyre backed throne set between two pink columns and flanked by the apostles. There is a niche set above the rock cut altar and to each side are painted curtains, known as a dado, giving the impression that the church had expensive fabrics decorating it.

In the vault is carved a large cross within a diamond. On the arch leading to the narthex, Christ is painted with two archangels, one on each side, and in the vault of the narthex stand rows of the twenty four elders of the apocalypse from the Book of Revelation, and below them the forty martyrs of Sebaste. All these figures are individually named.

On the west wall is the Last Judgement. This has four registers, with Christ in a mandorla presiding at the top above some of the forty martyrs. Beneath is the actual judgement with Saint Michael on the left weighing up someone's head or soul as the devil looks on.

An opening in the northwest corner leads to a funerary chapel with several burial spaces and an apse to the east. The painting on the north tympanum shows Christ standing on a footstool flanked by the Virgin and John the Baptist.

Crossing back over the bridge and turning right to follow the valley northwards, the most interesting church is signed and is a short steep walk up the valley side.

Kirkdamaltı kilise (Church of St George)

This irregularly shaped church has an unusual donor portrait on the west wall, the wall facing the apse. Saint George is in the centre flanked by a man in a turban on the left, the Emir Basil, and a woman carrying the model of a building on the right, his wife the Georgian princess Thamar. The church has been dated between 1282 and 1304. It was painted when the region was under Seljuk rule, and the inscription praises both the Byzantine emperor and the Seljuk sultan.

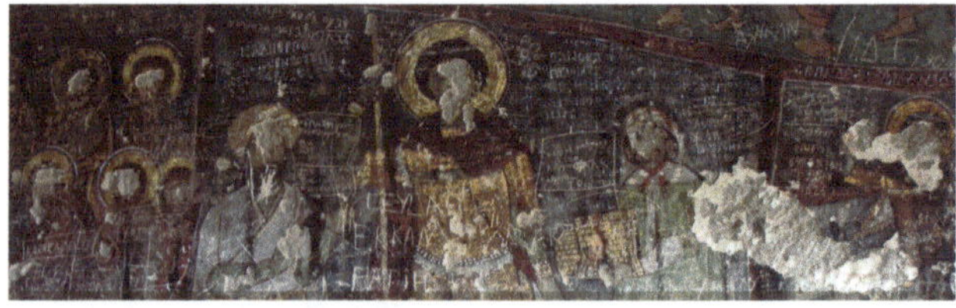

Saint George and donors, Kirkdamaltı kilise, Ihlara valley

Belisırma

Returning to the north of the valley, in the hills on the west side of the river valley across from Belisırma are two interesting churches, the Bahattin Samanlığı and Direkli Kilise. They have both recently been shut due to the stone cracking.

Direkli kilise (Church with the Columns)

This is an impressively large church with four massive piers supporting a dome. The width of the piers and the height of the dome make the bays of the cross-in-square design church appear steep and narrow. It is dated between 979 and 1025, but is probably around 1025 with the paintings of the saints on the piers dated to the end of the eleventh century. As you enter, there are saints painted on the faces of the piers facing you (the west face). These are the Virgin on the south one, to the right, and her mother, Anna, on the north, to the left. On the south east pier are the paired Saints Cosmas and Damion facing, on the north east pier, Saint Panteleimon. On this pier, facing the apse, are Sergios and Bakchos and on the north face, George.

In the apse is Christ with the Virgin, John the Baptist and angels.

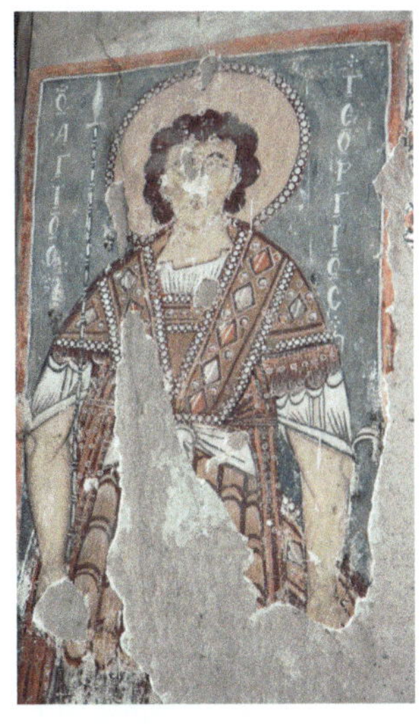

Saint George, Direkli kilise, Ihlara valley

George is dressed in elaborate military dress. His name is inscribed with the word Saint on one side and George on the other. Many saints in Byzantine art are depicted as young, perhaps alluding to how their short lives were cut off by their affiliation to Christ.

The patrons

The men and women who paid for the excavation and painting of churches in Cappadocia were often pictured, sometimes on their own but also with Christ or the Virgin, or their favourite saint. There are inscriptions, sometimes found on the cornice or around the apse, which record the names of the patrons, and usually the portraits also have inscriptions with short epithets naming the donors and expressing hope for their salvation. A popular phrase is, 'Entreaty of the servant of God,' followed by the person's name. Another common inscription is simply, 'Lord, help thy servant', again named. Occasionally there is a note to the viewer, such as, 'You who read this, pray for them'. The sense is that the donors are to be noted and remembered for their gifts to God and the belief that their beneficence will bring about salvation. Many of the donors of monastic churches are laymen and women. This was very popular in the large cities of the Byzantine empire, such as Constantinople and Thessaloniki, but also found throughout the smaller towns and villages. In Cappadocia, many of the donors are military men, like Michael Skepides at Karabaş Kilise.

Apocryphal stories

Stories about the life of Christ found in the Gospels were supplemented by tales found in apocryphal texts, which were very popular. These filled out the skeletal information and gave a very human and empathetic aspect to the narratives, while explaining some of the obscure or difficult features. The most well-known text was the *Infancy Gospel of Jacob*, which is the source for many of the scenes concerning the Virgin which appear in Cappadocian churches.

The Virgin

The Virgin's first steps are important for after this her feet never touch the ground, something which emphasises her purity. She is given to the high priest at the temple and seated on the altar, where an angel feeds her bread. She and the other virgins are given wool to spin and she receives the red yarn, a sign that she will bear a king. When her time to be betrothed comes, all the eligible men are given a stick, and from Joseph's stick a dove emerges or his stick buds, showing that he is the one to receive her. He takes her to his house where he has four sons, one of whom, Jacob, is often shown leading the donkey in the Journey to Bethlehem and the Flight to Egypt. When the Virgin becomes pregnant, her virtue and that of Joseph are questioned, so they are made to drink bitter water. If they are innocent they will be unharmed by it, which they are. While these scenes are found elsewhere in Byzantine art, it is in Cappadocia that they are most frequently used.

The Persecution of Elizabeth

In the apocrypha, Elizabeth flees with her son the future John the Baptist and cousin of Christ. She hides in a cave during the Massacre of the Innocents when all the male children under two years old are killed. This scene does not appear often in art, but it does in Cappadocia.

The Murder of Zacharias

According to a text added on to the *Infancy Gospel of Jacob*, Zacharias, the father of John the Baptist, who was the High Priest at the temple, was killed because he refused to say where John and Elizabeth were hiding. He is shown being murdered in the temple, another scene which is not found frequently but does occur in Cappadocia.

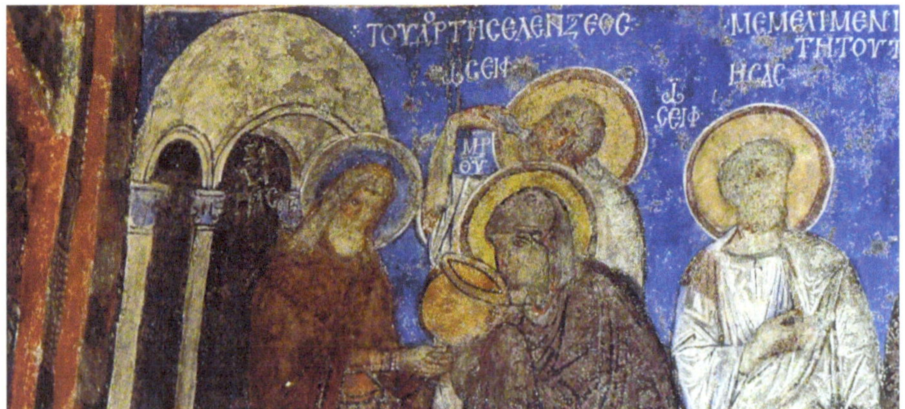

The Virgin tasting the Bitter Waters, Tokalı New Church, Göreme

CHAPTER SIX

ESKI GÜMÜSLER

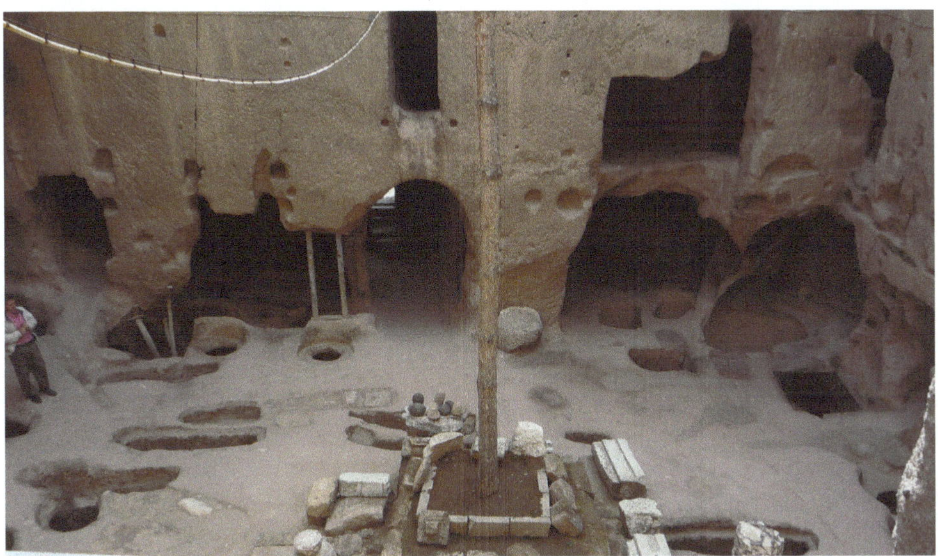

The monastery viewed from within the courtyard, looking back towards the entrance, Eski Gümüsler

About 80 kms south of Göreme is this impressive rock cut monastery established around a courtyard. The church lies on the north side of the courtyard and its facade clearly distinguishes it as the most important part of the complex with its tall blind arcade on which is carved a cross. This facade may well have been plastered and painted. You enter the building into the narthex which seems formal and rather splendid with similar blind arcades around the walls and a heavy cornice. Carved in relief in the south lunette is a cross and in the barrel vault a boss. The doorway in the east wall leading to the nave has heavy roll mouldings. To the right of this doorway the blind arcade has been cut back to create a recessed area on which is painted the Virgin and Child flanked by two angels. Entering the church, the massive columns are startling, partly because they have been darkened over time. The design is the standard cross-in-square plan with a small dome and barrel vaulted arms of the cross. Unlike many of the apses in Cappadocia which are horseshoe shaped, the three apses here are oval. To the north is a small chapel reached from the east bay of the church and to the left of this in the centre bay is a tomb recess with two graves.

The painting was restored in 1962-5 and is thought to come from three dates although this is not entirely clear. In the main

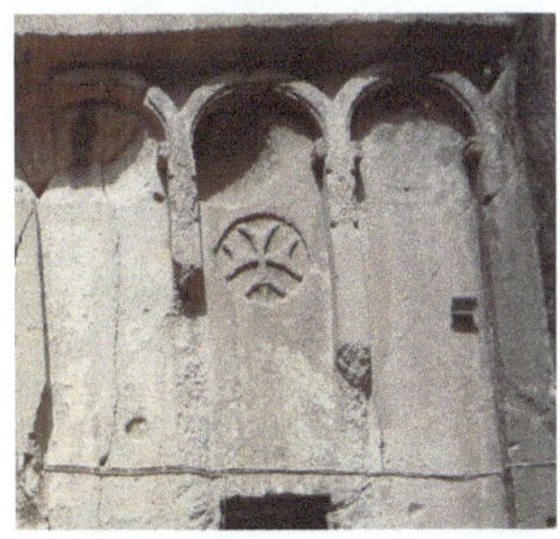

The sculpted façade of the courtyard at Eski Gümüsler

The entire centre of the site had to be excavated from above before the rooms themselves were excavated. Therefore when you walk in through the gateway at **Eski Gümüsler** you are enclosed in a courtyard with rock face on four sides within which are two or more levels of chambers with additional caves beneath the courtyard itself.

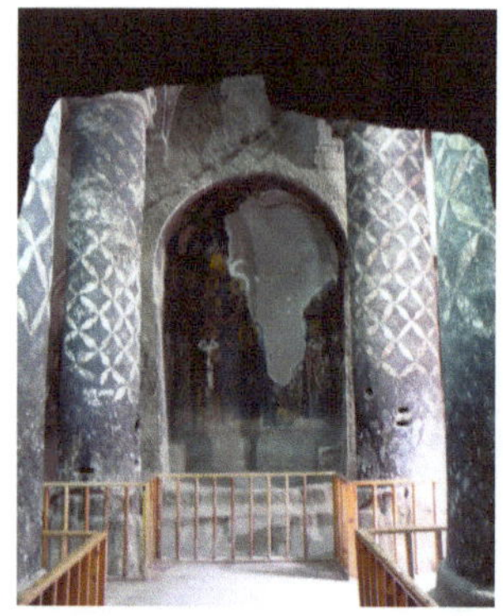

The church at Eski Gümüsler, facing the apse

The paintings in the church at **Eski Gümüsler** are probably from different dates and by **various artists**. It is worthwhile to look critically at paintings and examine the evidence for such suggestions.

apse is a *deisis* with Christ flanked by the Virgin and John the Baptist with apostles and bishops below. In the north apse is the Virgin and in the south John the Baptist. The only painted wall in the church is above the tomb recess and is arranged in three registers, with the Annunciation on either side of the niche, the Nativity above and the Presentation in the top register.

Michael Gough, who worked on the restoration, gives three painters, painter A who painted the narthex panel and the apse, painter B who painted the north wall, and painter C who painted the small apses. It has been suggested by Lyn Rodley that the difference may not indicate much variance in date but simply of artist and certainly the paintings in the side apses are of a far lower quality than the other painting. Does the narthex panel and apse seem to you to be painted by the same hand? Suggestions have been made as to when these were painted by comparison with other paintings. Nicole Thierry links the painting of the apse to another from probably 1025-8, and Lyn Rodley links the north wall painting to those at Karabaş kilise in the Soğanlı valley which was dated to 1060/61 (page 28). Therefore there is some 25 or 30 years between the two.

Above the church there is also an unsual painted room with scenes said to be from Aesop's fables, which are dated later.

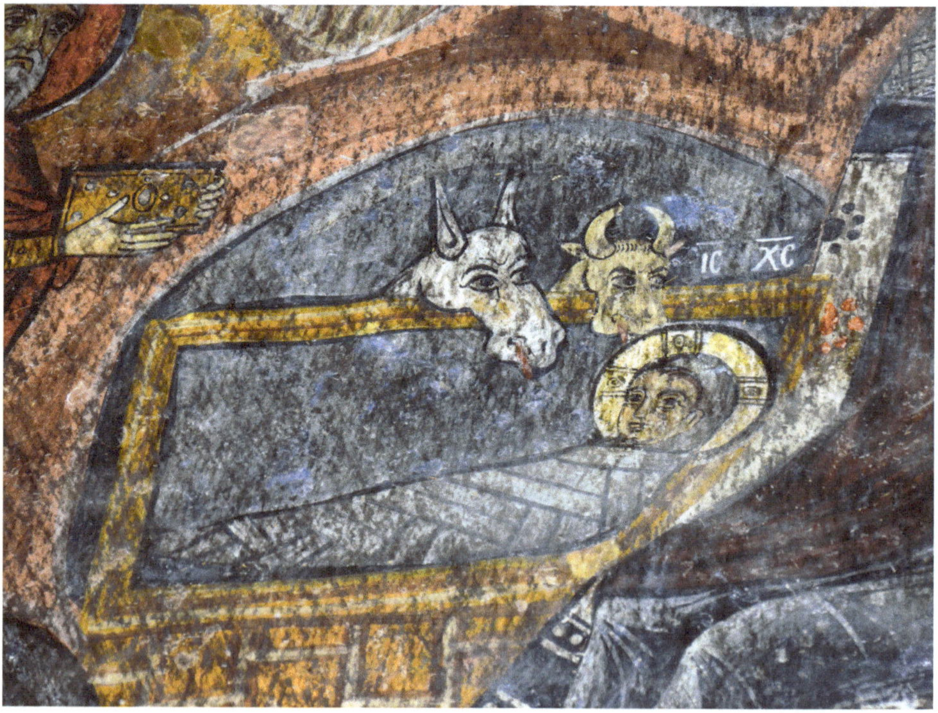

The Christ child, detail from the Nativity, Eski Gümüsler

CHAPTER SEVEN

FURTHER EXPLORATIONS

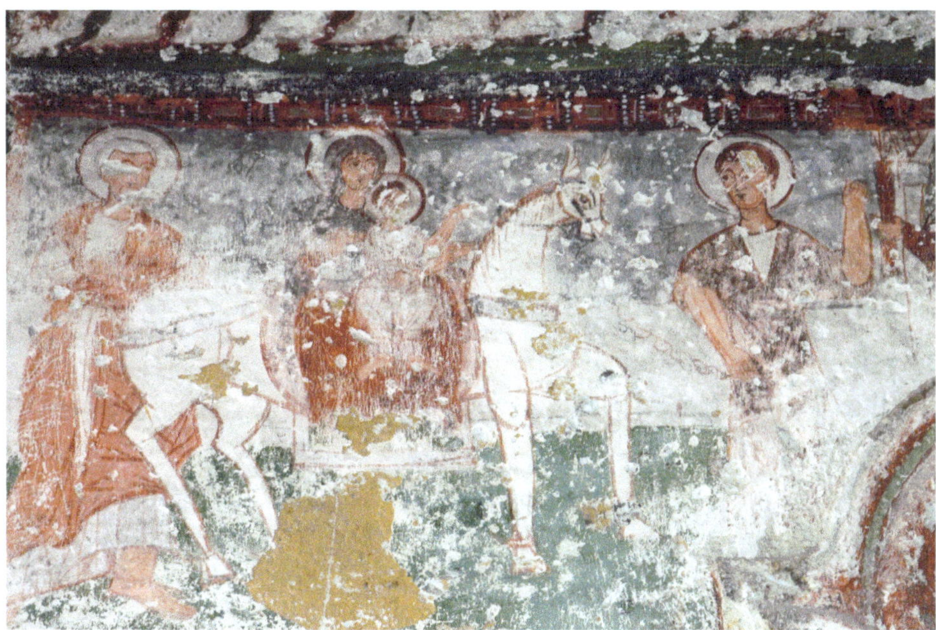

The Flight to Egypt, Pancarlık kilise

This chapter suggests some other sites which are well worth visiting in Cappadocia, near to Göreme. They are normally open and have fine paintings.

Keşlik Monastery, Cemil

This monastery is about 15 kms from Urgüp, just to the right of the road running south from Urgüp. There is a small entrance fee to visit the delightfully maintained site. It has two churches, one named after St Michael, the other after St Stephen.

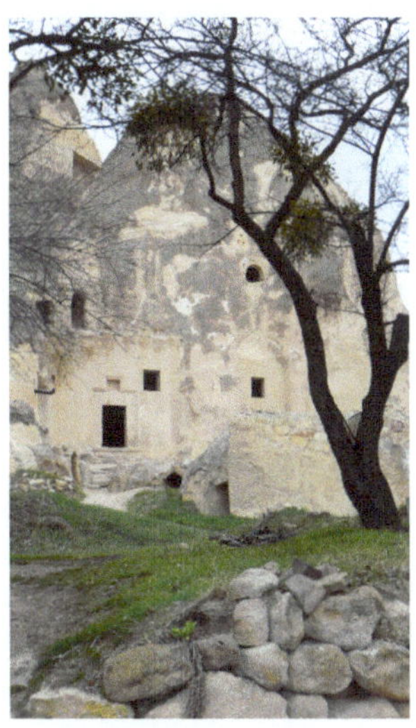

Keşlik monastery, Cemil

St Michael kilise

The eleventh-century paintings inside this rock cut church are very dark, discoloured by time and the smoke from candles and lamps. The door opens into the narthex where there are scenes from the apocryphal early life of the Virgin in the vault. On the walls of the main part of the church, and particularly in the right aisle, are scenes from Christ's life. There is a large, later representation of the archangel Michael on the wall facing the entry door.

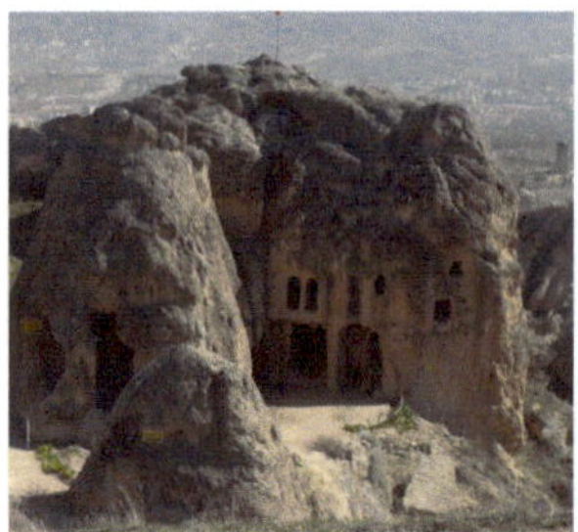

Pancarlık kilise and monastery

Pancarlık kilise is set in a broad and beautiful valley and is surrounded by monastic buildings. The **paintings** are graphic and distinct.

St Stephen kilise

This is accessed via a short path to the east of St Michael kilise. It is a small chapel with colourful nonrepresentational painted decoration. The ceiling is particularly rich, with intertwining foliate patterns. The dating of this space is controversial as it is sometimes attributed to the iconoclastic period (early-eighth to mid-ninth century), since it has no figural imagery. However, it is more likely to be later, perhaps tenth century, and is an example of how motifs from nature can be used for decorative purposes throughout the period.

Pancarlık Valley

This valley is accessed from the road leading southeast from Ortahisar, about 3 kms from the town.

There are two sites, one Sarıca, directly off the road has been developed as a tourist site, has a fee to visit, and is decorated with simple monochrome paintings. It is perhaps one of the least interesting sites.

Pancarlık kilise

Of much more interest is the church known as Pancarlık, dedicated to St Theodore. This is signposted and not far from the road. It is a monastic site, and the church is filled with iconographically rich paintings with strong rust coloured and green images with scenes from the Virgin's and Christ's lives.

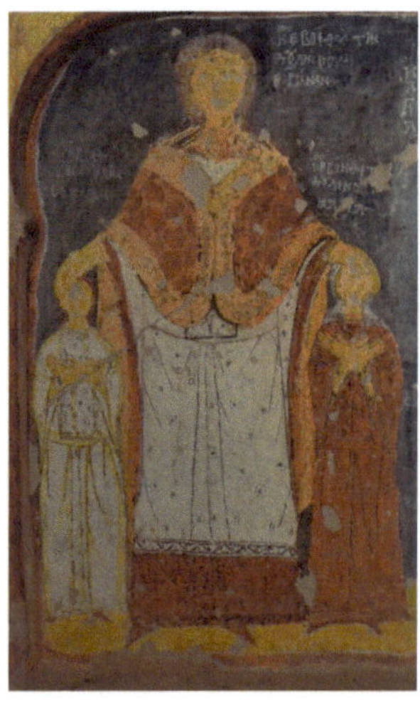

St John, Karsı Kilise, Gülşehir

At **St John**, a female patron of the church is depicted with two girls. In a similar painting a man is shown with two boys.

Gülşehir

St John, Karsı Kilise

This church is about a one hour drive from Göreme. It is on the right, 2.5 kms after the bridge on the Nevşehir road. It was renovated in 1212 and so the paintings are a little later than many visible in Cappadocia and were made when the region was under Seljuk rule. Throughout this period, religious practice, and patronage, was maintained despite changing political situations. Apart from a full array of the usual type of imagery, the church has two donor panels and a vivid and detailed Last Judgement.

Şahinefendi

The church of the Forty Martyrs

Located in the village of Şahinefendi, about 20 kms from Urgüp, this church is dedicated to the 40 martyrs of Sebaste, who died in a frozen lake. It is dated to 1216 and is a double church with two naves as well as a chapel beneath.

GLOSSARY

Anastasis: Means the 'Resurrection' and used to refer to the image of Christ breaking the gates of Hell and raising the dead

Aniconic: Non-figural imagery

Arcade: A series of arches supported by columns or piers

Barrel vault: A continuous arch which covers a space providing a ceiling or roof

Basileus: Principal title of the Byzantine emperor

Bema: Church sanctuary, normally at the east end of a church, which includes the area by the altar, behind the templon screen, and the area just in front

Blind arcade: A decorative row of arches attached to a wall

Byzantine: The term given to the empire and its culture that had Constantinople as its capital from 330 to 1453 CE

Christ Emmanuel: A form of Christ in which he is normally shown as a youth or boy

Christ Pantokrator: A form of Christ in which he is normally shown bearded with dark hair, holding a Gospel Book

Cornice: A horizontal decorative moulding on a building

Diakonikon: The area of a church to the right (usually south) of the sanctuary, used as a sacristy

Deisis: Literally a prayer or petition; used to refer to an image of Christ flanked by the Virgin and John the Baptist

Iconoclasm: In Byzantium used to refer to two periods; c. 730-787 and 815-842 in which figural religious imagery was condemned

Iconophiles: Those who supported the continued use of figural religious imagery

Iconoclasts: Those who condemned the use of figural religious imagery

Iconography: The subject matter of a painting

Iconostasis: A screen between the sanctuary and the nave on which icons are placed and which develops from the templon screen

Katholikon: The principle church in a monastery

Koimisis: Literally means 'sleeping'; the Dormition of the Virgin when her soul was purportedly taken to heaven

Lectionary: A book with selections from the Gospels with readings according to the liturgical year

Liturgy: The Eucharistic rite; the ritual of the church

Loros: Long scarf worn by emperors and empresses and archangels; it is wrapped around the body and hangs down to the side or in front

Lunette: a semi-circular area of wall beneath an arch

Narthex: Transverse vestibule or entranceway to a church, which appears like a hall running across the end of building, often at the west end if the altar is at the east

Nave or naos: The main part of the church

Parakklesion: Side chapel, often funerary

Pier: An upright support for a superstructure, often square or rectangular in shape

Proskynesis: Literally means 'prostration'; the act of kneeling in reverence, before an icon, sacred object, or people of power

Prothesis: The area of a church to the left (usually north) of the sanctuary

Seraphim: Six-winged beings

Soffit: The underside of an arch

Synthronon: A usually semicircular bench for clergy around the apse of an early Christian church

Tempera: Form of paint using egg-yolk

Templon or templon screen: Screen separating the sanctuary from the nave

Tetramorph: Symbols of the Four Evangelists, the four living Creatures mentioned in the Book of Ezekiel; each is represented as a creature, usually shown with wings, with Matthew as a man, Mark as a lion, Luke as an ox, and John as an eagle

Theotokos: Meaning the 'bearer/mother of God' and used for the Virgin Mary

Trinity: The iconography of Abraham receiving three visitors or angels, seen as the Trinity, the three persons of the Godhead (God the Father, Christ, the Holy Spirit)

Typikon: The charter and rules of a monastery

Vault: An arched form used to provide a ceiling or roof

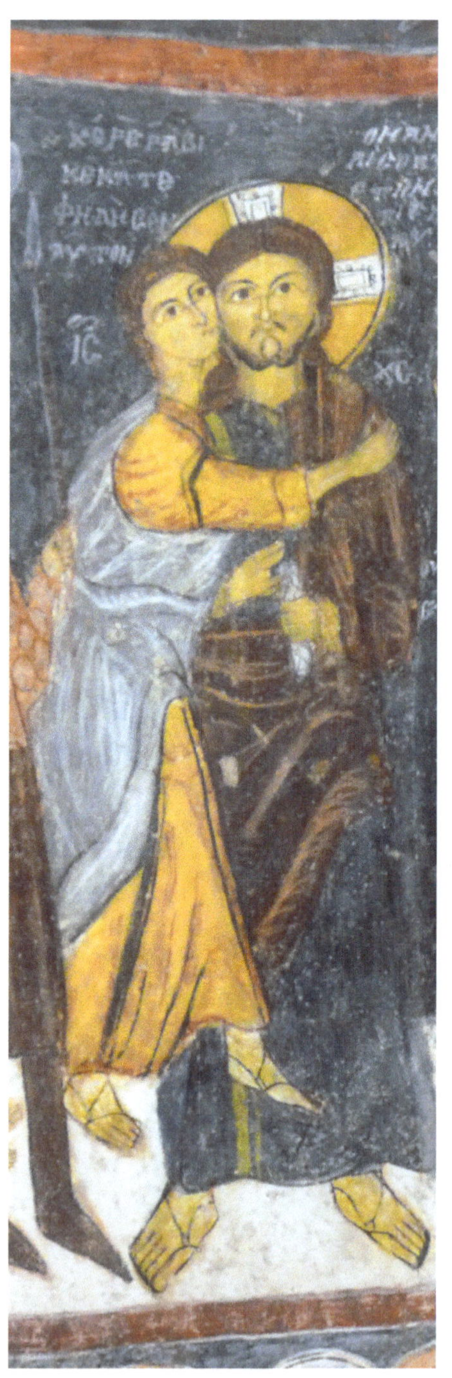

The Betrayal, St John kilise, Gülşehir

FURTHER READING

Academic books

Many of the books on Cappadocia are not in English, and there is relatively little which is really accessible both in terms of being in print and easily comprehensible to read. This selection gives the most important ones.

Jerphanion de, G. (1925-1942). *Les églises rupestres de Cappadoce.* 2 vols. in 4 parts, 3 vols. of plates. Paris, 1925-1942.
This, in French, is the classic text on the churches, still useful as a source for inscriptions and details.

Jolivet-Lévy, C. *La Cappadoce médiévale: images et spiritualité.* Photographs by Claude Sauvageot. Saint-Léger-Vauban, 2001.
This is an excellent book on the area and paintings.

Jolivet-Levy, C. *Sacred Art of Cappadocia. Byzantine Murals from the Sixth to 13th Centuries* (in colour with A. Ertug), Istanbul, 2006.
A stunning book with beautiful photographs and excellent text. A large investment.

Kostof, S. *Caves of God: Cappadocia and its Churches.* New York, 1989.
Good on the history and landscape and painting techniques.

Ousterhout, R. *A Byzantine Settlement in Cappadocia.* Washington, D.C., 2005.
Very interesting survey of an area with unparalleled details on daily life.

Restle, M. *The Byzantine wall painting in Asia Minor.* 3 vols. Recklinghausen, 1967.
Also, and more readily, available in German, very useful for building plans and identification of iconography.

Rodley, L. *Cave Monasteries of Cappadocia.* Cambridge, 1985.
Now reissued in paperback, this is invaluable for detailed analysis. Used extensively here for Nikephoros Phokas in Çavuşin, St Barbara and Karabaş churches in the Ihlara valley and the paintings at Eski Gümüsler.

Thierry, N. *Haut moyen-âge en Cappadoce: Les églises de la région de Çavuşin.* 2 vols. Paris, 1983 (I), 1994 (II).
In French, the most useful source for the area of Çavuşin.

Wharton, A. J. *Tokalı kilise: Tenth-century Metropolitan Art in Byzantine Cappadocia.* Washington, D. C., 1986.
Fairly accessible book on Tokalı kilise.

Guide books

The Rough Guide to Turkey.
Of the major guide books, this is the best at this time for Cappadocia, with good text and maps.

Oberheu, S. and M. Wadenpohl. *Cappadocia.* Noderstedt, 2010.
This is a useful guide to the region by local experts with good walking information.

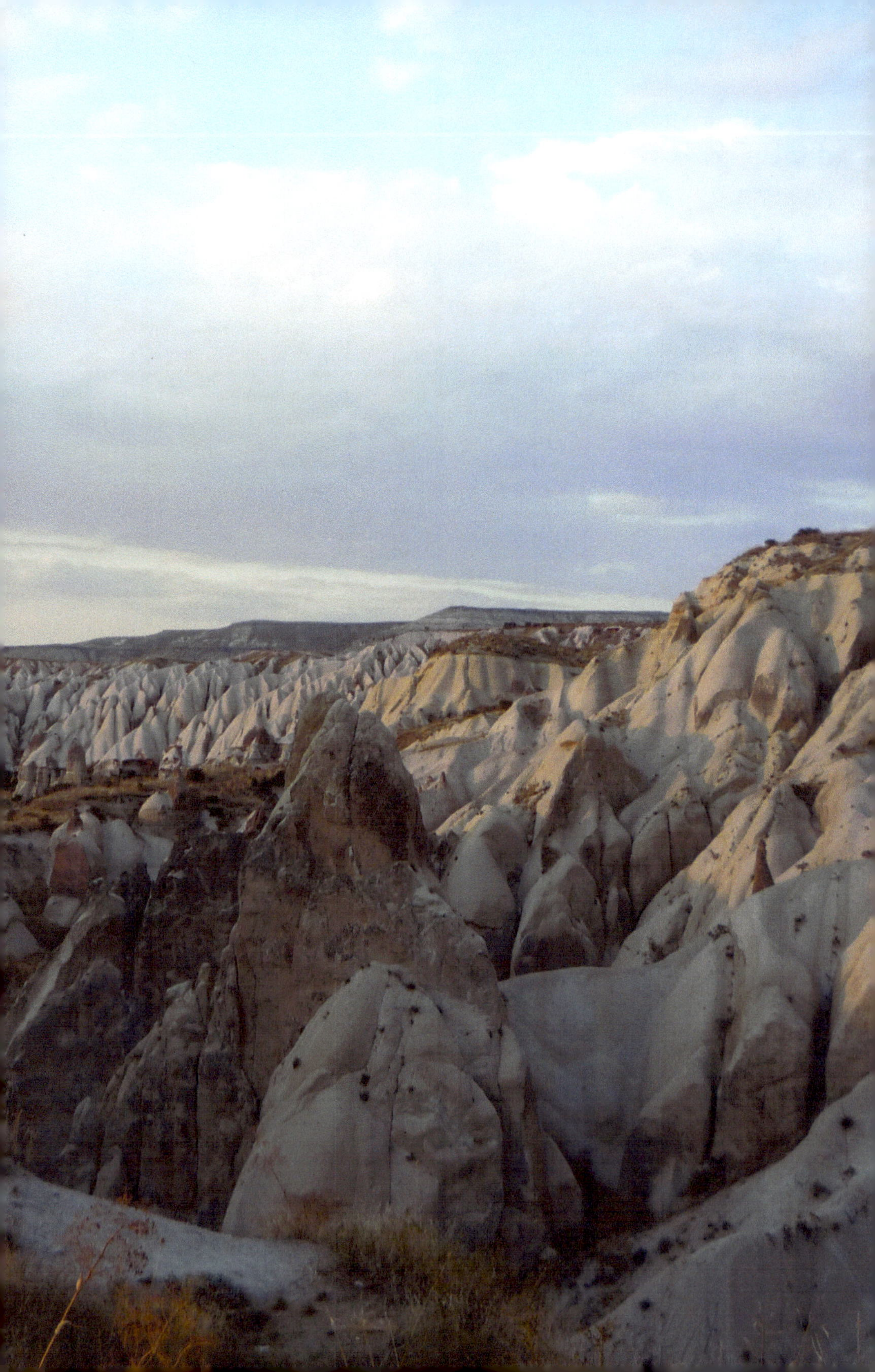

LIST OF FIGURES AND MAPS

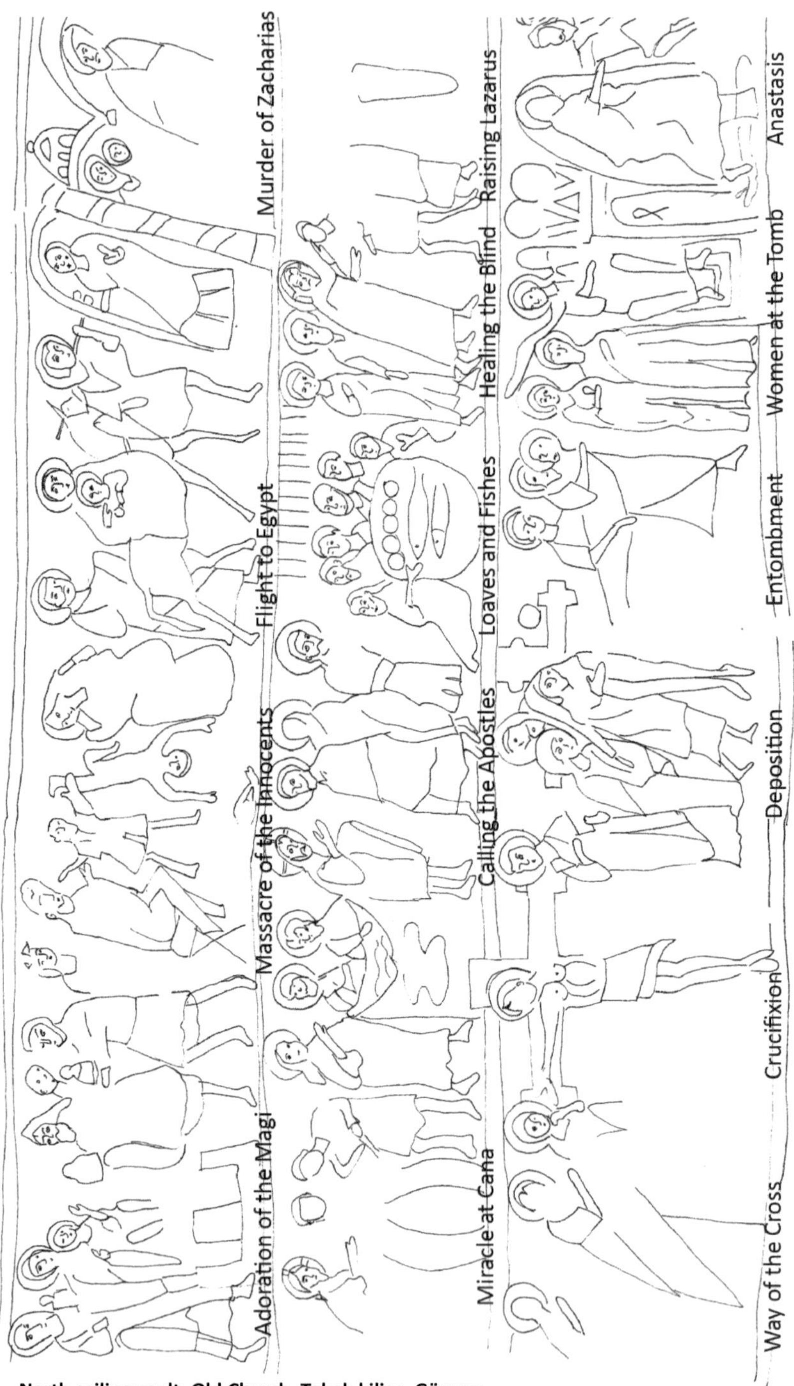

Figure 1 North ceiling vault, Old Church, Tokalı kilise, Göreme

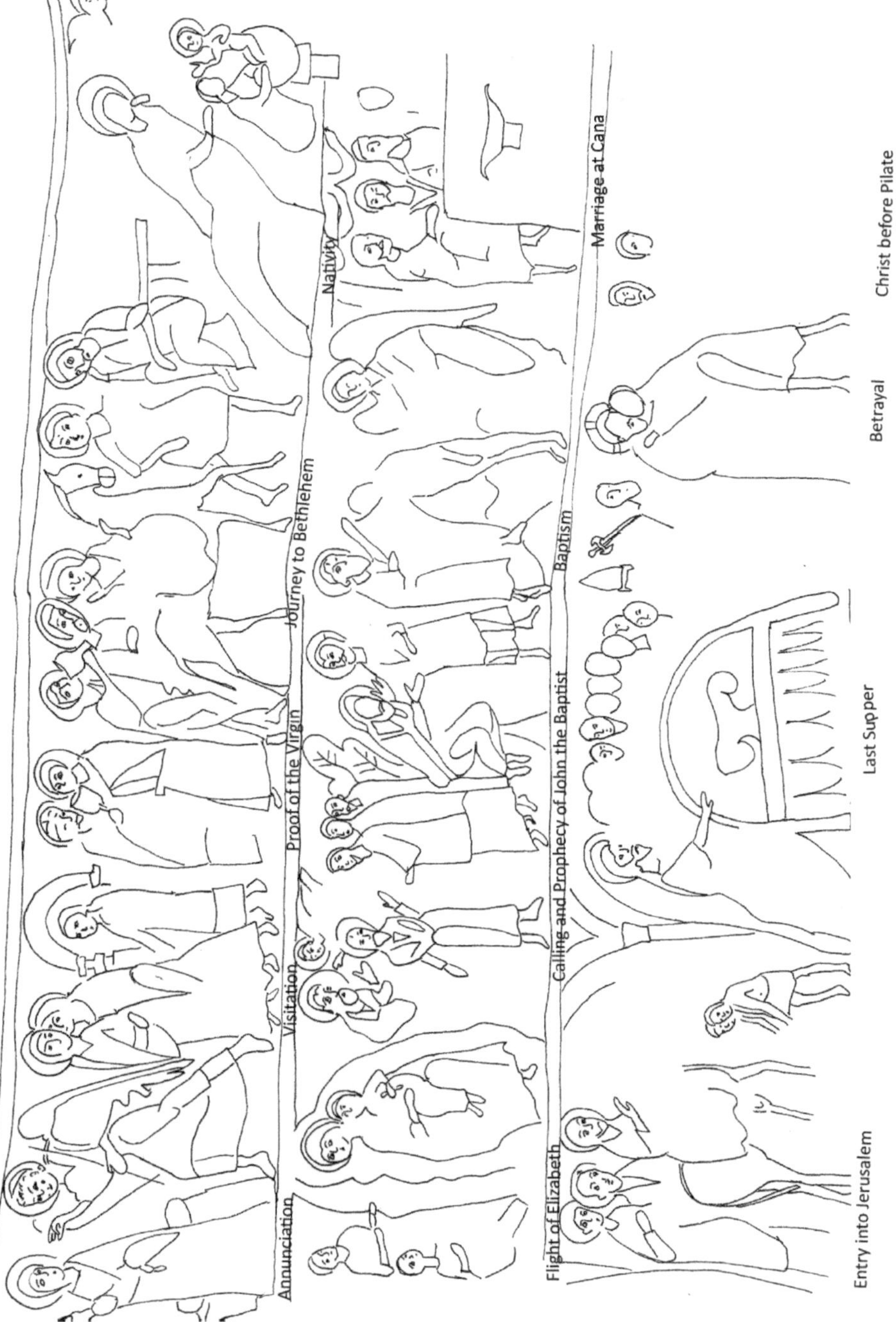

Figure 2 South ceiling vault, Old Church, Tokalı kilise, Göreme

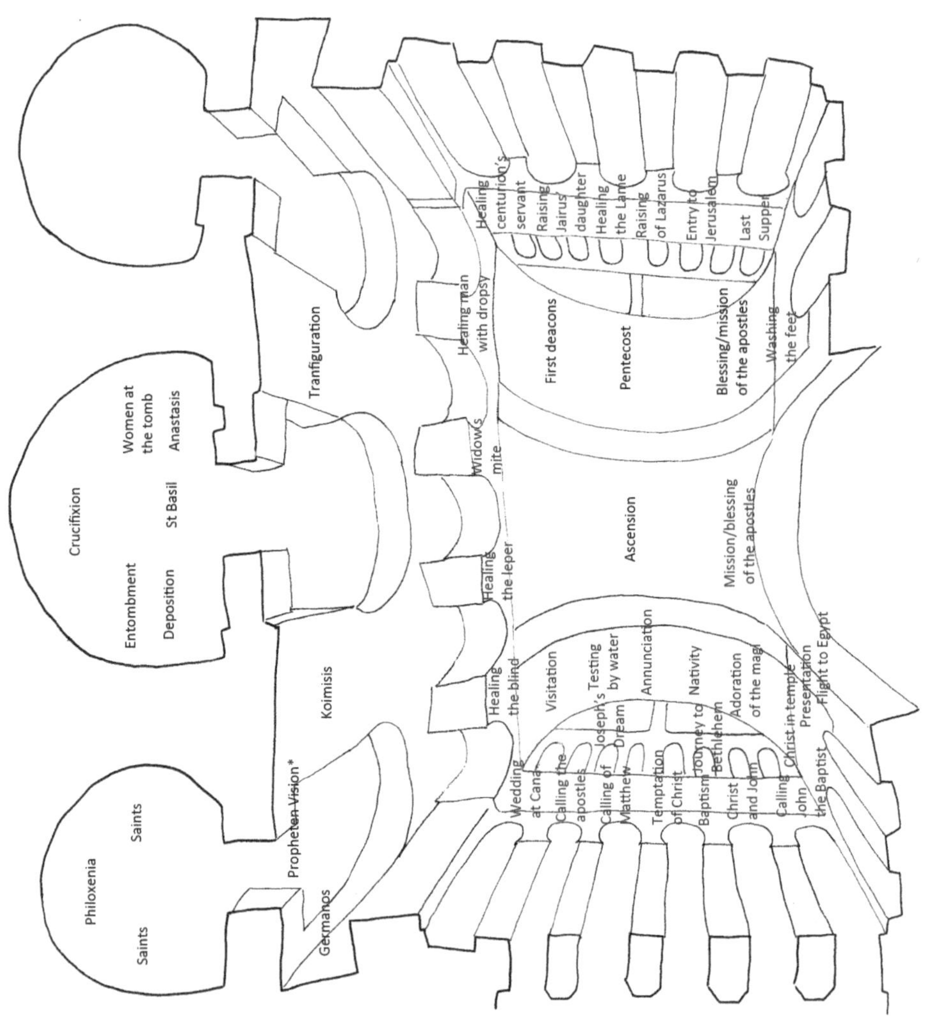

Figure 3 Plan with paintings, New Church, Tokalı kilise, Göreme

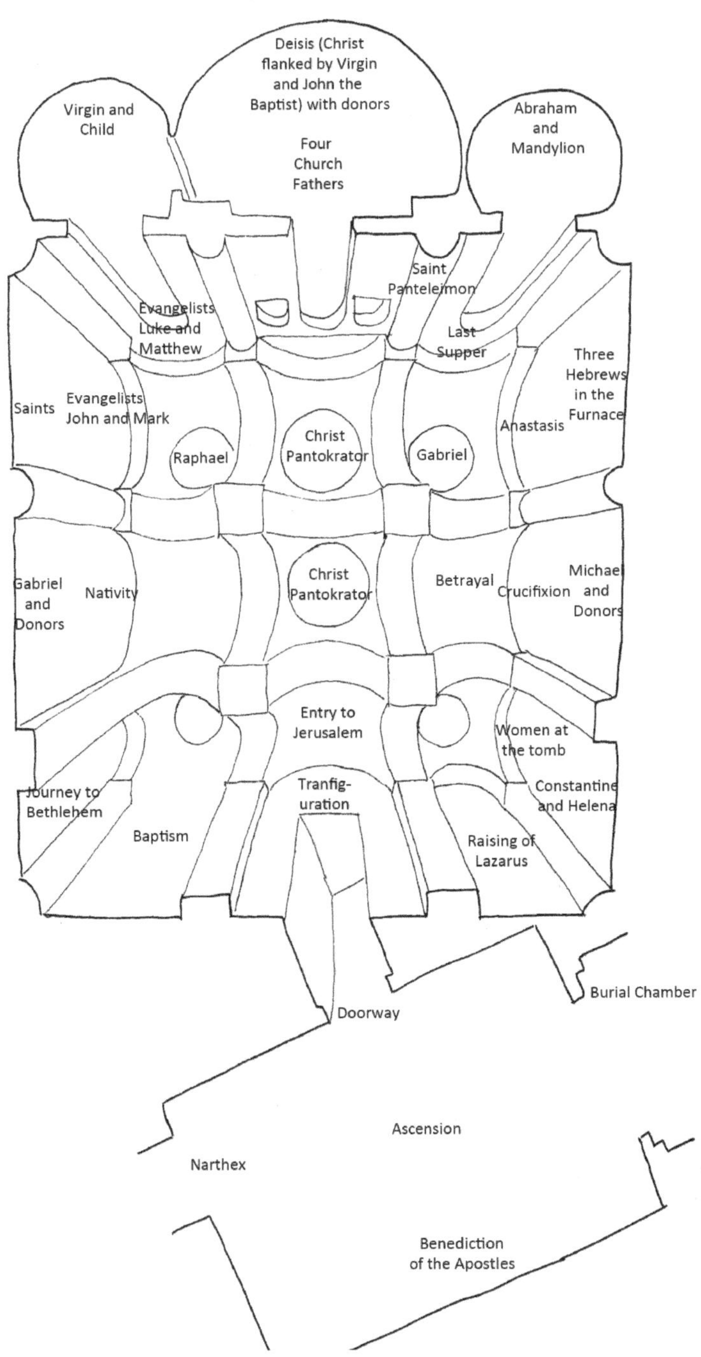

Figure 4 Plan with paintings, Karanlık kilise, Göreme

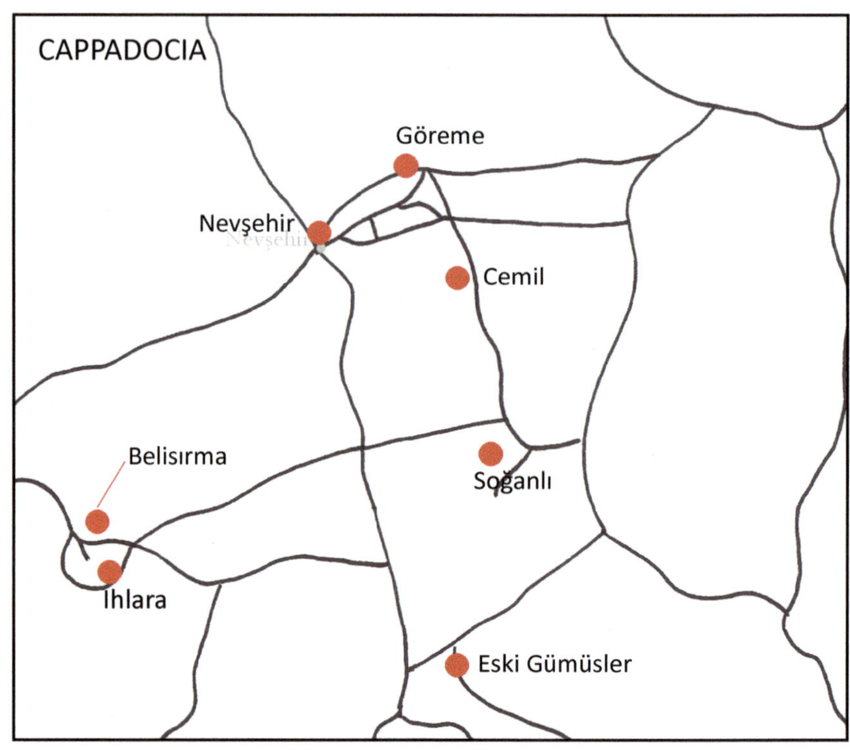

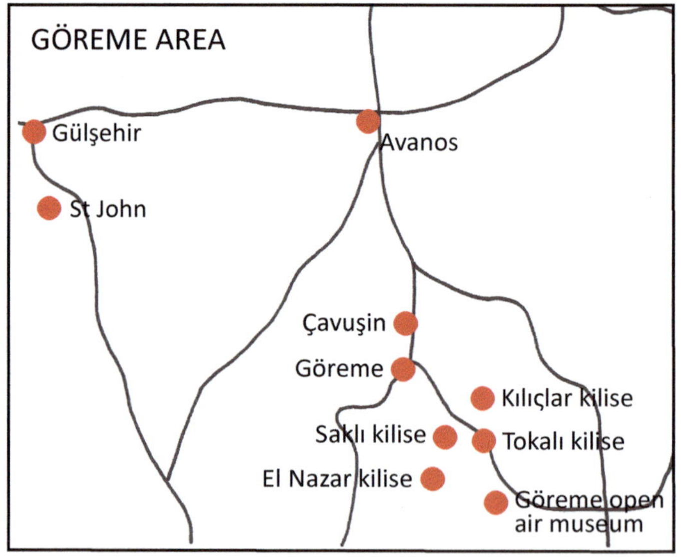

Figure 5 Map of Cappadocia

Figure 6 Map of Göreme area

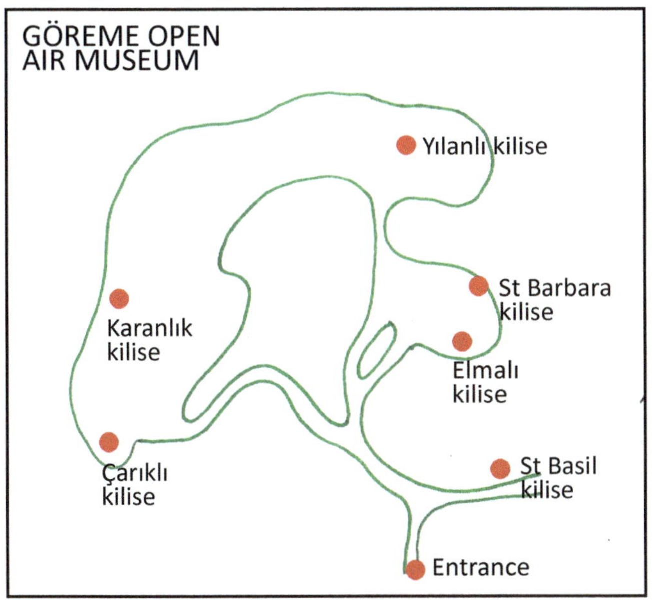

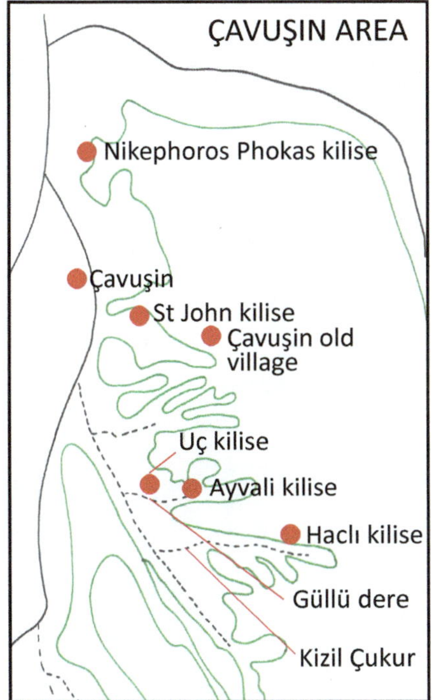

Figure 7 Map of Göreme Open Air Museum

Figure 8 Map of Çavuşin area

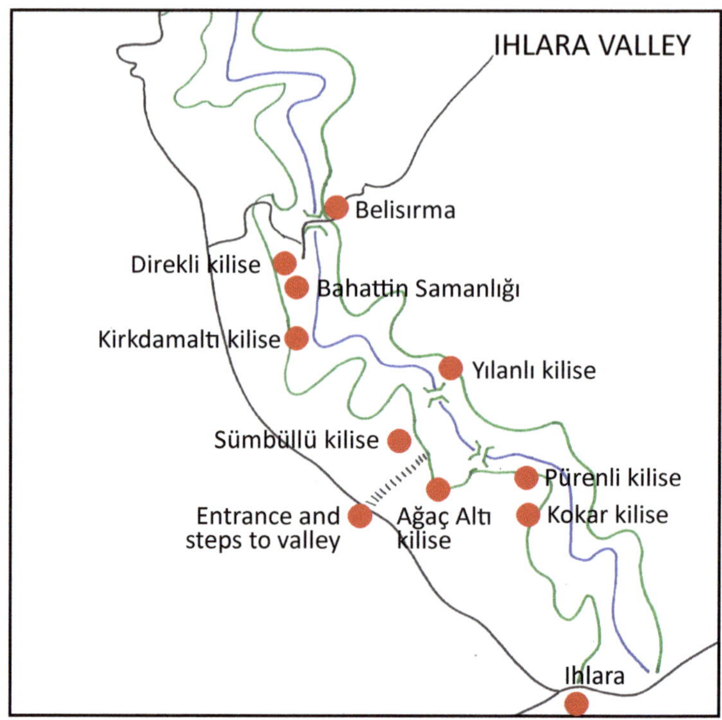

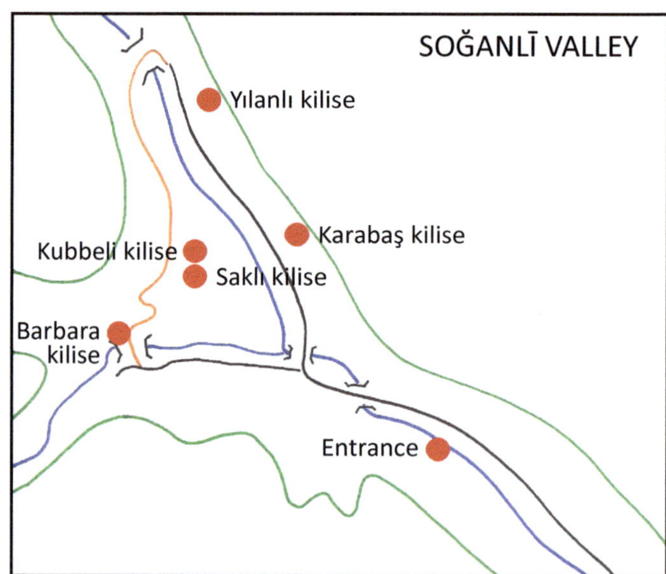

Figure 9 Map of Ihlara Valley

Figure 10 Map of Soğanlı Valley

INDEX

Numbers in **bold** indicate main entry, illustration or box feature.
Scenes from the bible (Old Testament and New Testament) and the apocrypha as well as saints are listed under Iconography.
Churches are listed under the valley or village which they are in or near.

www.ingramcontent.com/pod-product-compliance
Lightning Source LLC
LaVergne TN
LVHW052309100826
845147LV00006B/716